The Delia Collection
Chocolate

BBC BOOKS

Published by BBC Books
BBC Worldwide Ltd
Woodlands
80 Wood Lane
London W12 0TT

First published in 2003

A proportion of these recipes has been
published previously in *Delia Smith's Winter
Collection*, *Delia Smith's Summer Collection*,
Delia's How To Cook Books One, *Two* and *Three*,
*Delia Smith's Complete Illustrated Cookery
Course*, *Delia Smith's Christmas*, *Delia's Red Nose
Collection* and *Delia's Vegetarian Collection*.

Edited for BBC Worldwide Ltd
by New Crane Ltd

Editor: Sarah Randell
Designer: Paul Webster
Sub-editor: Heather Cupit
Picture Editor: Diana Hughes
Recipe Testing: Pauline Curran
Commissioning Editor for the BBC: Vivien Bowler

ISBN 0 563 487321

Printed and bound in Italy
by L.E.G.O SpA
Colour separation by Radstock Reproductions Ltd
Midsomer Norton

Cover and title-page photographs: Michael Paul
For further photographic credits, see page 136

Introduction

When I look back over my years of cookery writing, I have to admit that very often, decisions about what to do have sprung from what my own particular needs are. As a very busy person who has to work, run a home and cook, I felt it was extremely useful to have, for instance, summer recipes in one book – likewise winter and Christmas, giving easy access to those specific seasons.

This, my latest venture, has come about for similar reasons. Thirty three years of recipe writing have produced literally thousands of recipes. So I now feel what would be really helpful is to create a kind of ordered library (so I don't have to rack my brains and wonder which book this or that recipe is in!). Thus, if I want to make a chocolate recipe, I don't have to look through the chocolate sections of various books, but have the whole lot in one convenient collection.

In compiling these collections I have chosen what I think are the best and most popular recipes and, at the same time, have added some that are completely new. It is my hope that those who have previously not tried my recipes will now have smaller collections to sample, and that those dedicated followers will appreciate an ordered library to provide easy access and a reminder of what has gone before and may have been forgotten.

Delia Smith

Conversion Tables

All these are approximate conversions, which have either been rounded up or down. In a few recipes it has been necessary to modify them very slightly. Never mix metric and imperial measures in one recipe, stick to one system or the other.

All spoon measurements used throughout this book are level unless specified otherwise.

All butter is salted unless specified otherwise.

All recipes have been double-tested, using a standard convection oven. If you are using a fan oven, adjust the cooking temperature according to the manufacturer's handbook.

Weights

½ oz	10 g
¾	20
1	25
1½	40
2	50
2½	60
3	75
4	110
4½	125
5	150
6	175
7	200
8	225
9	250
10	275
12	350
1 lb	450
1 lb 8 oz	700
2	900
3	1.35 kg

Volume

2 fl oz	55 ml
3	75
5 (¼ pint)	150
10 (½ pint)	275
1 pint	570
1¼	725
1¾	1 litre
2	1.2
2½	1.5
4	2.25

Dimensions

⅛ inch	3 mm
¼	5
½	1 cm
¾	2
1	2.5
1¼	3
1½	4
1¾	4.5
2	5
2½	6
3	7.5
3½	9
4	10
5	13
5¼	13.5
6	15
6½	16
7	18
7½	19
8	20
9	23
9½	24
10	25.5
11	28
12	30

Oven temperatures

Gas mark	°F	°C
1	275°F	140°C
2	300	150
3	325	170
4	350	180
5	375	190
6	400	200
7	425	220
8	450	230
9	475	240

Contents

Cakes

Chocolate Fudge Cake
Serves 6-8

For the cake

6 oz (175 g) self-raising wholemeal flour

1 rounded teaspoon baking powder

6 oz (175 g) very soft butter

6 oz (175 g) light soft brown sugar

3 large eggs, at room temperature

1 rounded tablespoon cocoa powder

For the chocolate fudge filling and topping

4½ oz (125 g) light soft brown sugar

a 170 g tin of evaporated milk

4½ oz (125 g) dark chocolate (50-55 per cent cocoa solids), broken into small pieces

2 oz (50 g) soft butter

2 drops of vanilla extract

To decorate

whole almonds, dusted with cocoa powder or icing sugar

You will also need two 7 inch (18 cm) sponge tins, 1½ inches (4 cm) deep, lightly greased, and the bases lined with baking parchment.

Pre-heat the oven to gas mark 3, 325°F (170°C).

This recipe was born in the Seventies, when there was a sudden surge of partiality for things healthy and 'whole'. The problem was, 'whole' sometimes meant heavy. Not so with this one, though, as the wholemeal flour gives an extra special moistness to the cake.

First of all, weigh the flour, then take out 1 rounded tablespoon of flour and replace it with the rounded tablespoon of cocoa. The tablespoon of flour you take out won't be needed. Now simply take a very large mixing bowl, place the flour, baking powder and cocoa in a sieve and sift it into the bowl, holding the sieve high to give it a good airing as it goes down. Now all you do is simply add the remaining cake ingredients to the bowl and beat them together. What you will end up with is a mixture that drops off a spoon when you give it a tap on the side of the bowl. If the mixture seems a little too stiff, add a little water and mix again.

Now divide the mixture and spread it evenly in the prepared tins and bake on the centre shelf of the oven for about 30-35 minutes or until springy in the centre. After 30 seconds (or thereabouts), turn the cakes out on to a wire cooling rack and strip off the base papers. Leave to cool while you make the chocolate fudge filling and topping.

To do this, combine the sugar and evaporated milk in a heavy saucepan. Heat gently to dissolve the sugar, stirring frequently. When the sugar has dissolved and the mixture comes to the boil, keep the heat very low and simmer for 6 minutes without stirring. Remove the pan from the heat and, using a small balloon whisk, whisk in the chocolate, followed by the butter and vanilla extract. Transfer the mixture to a bowl and, when it is cool, cover it with clingfilm and chill for about an hour to allow the mixture to thicken. Then beat again, and spread half on one sponge, placing the other one on top. Use the rest to spread over the top and sides and decorate the top with the almonds.

Cheat's Chocolate Rum Gateau
Serves 8

a ready-made chocolate loaf cake

4 tablespoons good-quality hazelnut chocolate spread

2 fl oz (55 ml) dark rum

1 oz (25 g) whole, blanched hazelnuts

15 fl oz (425 ml) double cream

1 tablespoon icing sugar, sifted

Pre-heat the oven to gas mark 4, 350°F (180°C).

This recipe, originally invented for Comic Relief, is the busy person's chocolate dessert, which is made in an instant but tastes like you slaved all day. It freezes like a dream – so why not whip up two of them while you're at it?

Begin by toasting the hazelnuts on a baking sheet on the top shelf of the oven for 7 minutes, using a timer. After that, roughly chop them, then remove the paper from the cake, turn it on its side on a board and, using a serrated knife, cut it lengthways into 5 slices. Then arrange the slices on the board in the order you cut them (as you'll be reassembling them into their original shape a little later).

Next, brush rum all over the cake slices, making sure it's all used up. Then, in a bowl, whip the cream with the icing sugar until quite stiff, using an electric hand whisk. Spread 4 layers of the cake (not the top one) with the chocolate spread, then spread the same 4 layers with about 4 heaped tablespoons of the cream. After that, layer the cake back together, pressing the top down lightly. Now cover the whole lot with the remaining cream and finally, sprinkle with the hazelnuts. Cover and chill for about 3 hours before serving.

Bûche de Noël (chocolate chestnut log)
Serves 8-10

For the base

6 large eggs

5 oz (150 g) golden caster sugar

2 oz (50 g) cocoa powder, sifted

a little icing sugar for dusting

For the filling

a 250 g tin crème de marrons
(sweetened chestnut purée)

4 whole marrons glacés (candied
chestnuts), roughly chopped

For the Christmas snow decoration

2 oz (50 g) dark chocolate
(70-75 per cent cocoa solids)

10 fl oz (275 ml) double cream,
less 1 tablespoon, for the filling
(see recipe)

You will also need a Swiss-roll tin
9 x 13 inches (23 x 32 cm), greased,
and lined with baking parchment,
and a few holly leaves.

Pre-heat the oven to gas mark 4,
350°F (180°C).

This famous French confection turns up in a number of guises, some of which I have a great aversion to, having never liked the sickly sweet butter cream that's often used for the icing. However, I do have a great passion for more sophisticated chocolatey chestnut recipes, so here I'm offering a lighter version, which also makes an excellent party cake.

First, make the base by separating the eggs – put the whites in a large, grease-free bowl and the yolks in a smaller bowl. Then, using an electric hand whisk, whisk the egg yolks until they start to pale and thicken, add the caster sugar and continue to whisk until the mixture becomes more thickened (do not overdo this or it will go too stiff). Now whisk in the cocoa powder until it's thoroughly blended in. Next, wash the whisk heads in warm, soapy water and, when they are absolutely dry, clean and grease free, whisk the egg whites until they form soft peaks. Spoon one lot of egg white into the chocolate mixture to loosen it, then begin carefully to fold all the chocolate mixture into the egg whites, cutting and folding until they're thoroughly combined. Spread the mixture into the prepared tin, giving it a few taps to even it out, and bake it in the centre of the oven for about 20 minutes or until it is risen and puffy and feels springy in the centre – it's important not to overcook it. When you take it out of the oven it will sink down quite a lot but that's quite in order, so don't panic. Let it cool completely, then place a sheet of baking parchment, about 1 inch (2.5 cm) larger all round than the Swiss-roll tin, on a work surface, and sprinkle it with some icing sugar. Loosen the edges of the chocolate base all round, turn it out on to the paper and carefully peel off the base paper.

Now for the filling: simply empty the contents of the chestnut purée into a bowl, add 1 tablespoon of double cream and mix thoroughly. Then, using a small palette knife, spread the mixture carefully and evenly all over the base. After that, sprinkle the chopped candied chestnuts all over. The next thing you need to do is have ready a plate that the whole length of the log will sit comfortably on (an oval meat plate can be used or you could line a small oblong tray with foil). Now, taking the edge of the baking parchment to guide you, roll the base over lengthways into a long roll, keeping it on the edge of the paper; then, transferring it to the plate, pull away the last of the paper. If it cracks or loses its shape, don't worry: just pat it back into a log shape, using your hands – nothing will show because of the topping. (If you want to freeze it at this stage, keep it in the paper, then wrap it in foil.) Now, to make an authentic-looking log, you need to cut 2 diagonal pieces off each end; these are to represent branches and should be about 2 inches (5 cm) at their widest part. Place one on one side of the log, cut side to join the log, and the other on the other side, but this time nearer the top. You'll find the sticky chestnut cream will make these two weld on to the rest okay. Now you have a log shape, all you require is some Christmas snow. For this, you need to melt the chocolate in a bowl over some hot water, then beat the rest of the 10 fl oz (275 ml) cream till it's spreadable – be careful not to overbeat. Now spread the cream evenly all over the log. Then drizzle a little trickle of the melted chocolate up and down the length of the cream, take a fork and, working only lengthways, blend the chocolate lightly into the cream, giving a woody, bark-like effect. The 'branches' need the chocolate swirled round with the fork at the ends, as do the ends of the log. I also like to put fresh holly on the plate.

Chocolate Beer Cake
Serves 8

For the cake

2 oz (50 g) cocoa powder

7 fl oz (200 ml) stout

4 oz (110 g) very soft butter

10 oz (275 g) dark soft brown sugar

2 large eggs, beaten

6 oz (175 g) plain flour

¼ teaspoon baking powder

1 teaspoon bicarbonate of soda

For the icing

4 oz (110 g) icing sugar, sifted

2 oz (50 g) very soft butter

2 tablespoons stout

4 oz (110 g) dark chocolate (50-55 per cent cocoa solids)

1 oz (25 g) walnut pieces, finely chopped

To decorate

8 walnut halves, dusted with cocoa powder

You will also need two 8 inch (20 cm) sponge tins, 1½ inches (4 cm) deep, lightly greased, and the bases lined with baking parchment lightly greased.

Pre-heat the oven to gas mark 4, 350°F (180°C).

If you come from Dublin, you make this with Guinness; if you come from Cork, you make this with Murphy's. Either way, the beer gives it an interesting and quite different flavour. We serve it in the supporters' club on match days in big, thick slices, as it has tons of man appeal.

First of all, cream the butter and sugar together, beating thoroughly for 3 or 4 minutes until pale and fluffy. Now gradually beat in the eggs, a little at a time, beating well between each addition. Next, sift the flour, baking powder and bicarbonate of soda on to a sheet of baking parchment. Then weigh the cocoa and put it in a separate bowl, gradually stirring the stout into it. Now carefully and lightly fold into the egg mixture small quantities of the sifted flour alternately with the cocoa-stout liquid. Then, when both have been added, divide the cake mixture equally between the 2 tins and level it out.

Bake the sponges in the centre of the oven for 30-35 minutes. The cakes should be flat on top and feel springy and will have shrunk slightly from the side of the tin. Leave them to cool in the tins for 5 minutes before turning out on to a wire rack to cool further, carefully stripping off the base papers.

To make the icing, beat the icing sugar and butter together until blended, then gradually add the stout, making sure it is thoroughly mixed in after each addition. Now melt the chocolate in a bowl set over hot water, making sure the bottom of the bowl doesn't touch the water. Then, when it's melted, remove the bowl from the water, and carefully fold the chocolate into the icing mixture. Now remove a third of the icing to a separate bowl and stir in the chopped walnuts. After all the icing has cooled to a spreadable consistency, sandwich the cake with the walnut icing. Then spread the remaining two-thirds of the icing on top of the cake, using a palette knife. Next, arrange the walnut halves on top of the cake. Now try to be patient and allow the icing to become firm before eating!

Chocolate Ricotta Cheesecake
Serves 8-10

For the base

2 oz (50 g) unblanched whole almonds

6 oz (175 g) plain chocolate oatmeal biscuits

1 oz (25 g) Grape-Nuts cereal

2 oz (50 g) butter, melted

For the cheesecake

5 oz (150 g) dark chocolate (70-75 per cent cocoa solids), broken into small pieces

12 oz (350 g) ricotta, at room temperature

7 fl oz (200 ml) half-fat crème fraîche, at room temperature

2 large eggs, separated

2 oz (50 g) golden caster sugar

3 leaves gelatine

2 tablespoons milk

To decorate

4 oz (110 g) dark chocolate (70-75 per cent cocoa solids) for the chocolate curls (see page 131)

a dusting of cocoa powder, to finish

You will also need an 8 inch (20 cm) diameter springform tin, sides and base lightly oiled with groundnut or other flavourless oil.

Pre-heat the oven to gas mark 6, 400°F (200°C).

This cheesecake is not intensely 'in-your-face' chocolatey, but more subtle. The texture and the slight acidity in the ricotta gives this an unusual edge and this, combined with the pure chocolate on top, is what makes it a very classy cheesecake.

First of all, spread the almonds out on a small baking sheet and toast them in the oven for 7 minutes, using a timer. After that, chop them quite finely. Next, place the biscuits in a plastic food bag and crush them, using a rolling pin. Then tip the crumbs into a mixing bowl, adding the chopped nuts and Grape-Nuts. Now add the melted butter to bind it all together, then press the mixture into the base of the tin, pop it into the oven and bake for 10 minutes. After that, remove it and leave it to cool.

Meanwhile, melt the 5 oz (150 g) of chocolate in a heatproof bowl over a pan of barely simmering water, making sure the base of the bowl doesn't touch the water, then remove it from the heat and let it cool as well. Next, in a large mixing bowl, whisk together the ricotta, crème fraîche, egg yolks and sugar until smooth and well blended. Now soak the leaves of gelatine in a small bowl of cold water for about 5 minutes and, while that's happening, heat the milk in a small saucepan up to simmering point before taking it off the heat. Squeeze the excess water from the gelatine, then add it to the milk and whisk until it has dissolved. Now stir the gelatine and milk, along with the cooled chocolate, into the ricotta mixture, until it is all thoroughly blended. Now, in another bowl and using clean beaters, whisk the egg whites to the soft-peak stage. Then first fold a tablespoon of egg white into the cheesecake mixture to loosen it, and then carefully but thoroughly fold in the rest of the egg white. Next, pour the mixture on to the prepared base, cover with clingfilm and chill in the fridge for at least 4 hours (even overnight – the longer the better). To unmould the cheesecake, first run a palette knife around the edge of the tin, then release the spring clip and remove it. After that, carefully lift off the base and transfer to a serving plate. Decorate with chocolate curls and give them a light dusting of sifted cocoa powder.

Note This recipe contains raw eggs.

Chocolate and Hazelnut Brownie Cake
Serves 8-10

For the cake

2 oz (50 g) dark chocolate
(70-75 per cent cocoa solids)

4 oz (110 g) chopped toasted hazelnuts

4 oz (110 g) butter

2 large eggs, lightly beaten

8 oz (225 g) golden granulated sugar

2 oz (50 g) plain flour

1 teaspoon baking powder

¼ teaspoon salt

To decorate

10 fl oz (275 ml) whipping or double cream

extra toasted nuts, roughly chopped

cocoa powder, to dust

You will also need a baking tin, 6 x 10 inches (15 x 25.5 cm) and 1 inch (2.5 cm) deep, the base and sides lined with parchment paper. Make sure that the paper stands up at least an inch (2.5 cm) above the edge of the tin.

Pre-heat the oven to gas mark 4, 350°F (180°C).

Be warned, this is wickedly rich — a chewy, chocolatey, nutty mixture sandwiched together with whipped cream. Great with hazelnuts but you can use other nuts like brazils, or even a mixture.

Place the chocolate and butter together in a large, heatproof bowl fitted over a saucepan of barely simmering water, and allow the chocolate to melt, making sure the base of the bowl doesn't touch the water. Then beat the mixture till smooth, remove it from the heat and simply stir in all the other ingredients till thoroughly blended. Now spread the mixture evenly into the prepared tin and bake on the centre shelf for 30 minutes. Leave the cake in the tin for 15 minutes to cool, then remove it from the tin, and turn it out on to a cooling tray. Strip off the lining paper and, when it's absolutely cold, carefully cut the cake in half, down the centre lengthways, so you're left with 2 oblongs.

Now whip the cream until it forms soft peaks and spread half of it thickly along one half. Position the other half on top, and then spread the rest of the cream all over the cake, covering it completely. Then decorate with the roughly chopped nuts and, if you like, a dusting of cocoa powder. If all the cake isn't eaten, to keep it fresh, store inside a polythene container in the fridge.

Squidgy Chocolate Cakes with Prunes in Marsala
Serves 4

For the cakes

½ oz (10 g) cocoa powder, plus a little extra for dusting

3 large eggs

1 tablespoon golden granulated sugar

a little groundnut or other flavourless oil for greasing

For the filling

12 ready-to-eat vanilla or other prunes

1½ fl oz (40 ml) Marsala

2 rounded tablespoons crème fraîche

1 teaspoon golden granulated sugar

1 tablespoon grated dark chocolate (70-75 per cent cocoa solids)

You will also need 4 ramekins, 1½ inches (4 cm) deep, with a base measurement of 3 inches (7.5 cm), very lightly greased, and a small baking tray.

The very lightest chocolate cakes of all are made without flour. This is the first version, but there are more to follow.

First of all, deal with the prunes by placing them in a small saucepan, together with the Marsala, then just bring them up to simmering point and leave to cool. Transfer them to a small, lidded plastic box and leave to soak for as long as possible, turning them now and then. (I always try to let them soak overnight.) When you're ready to make the cakes, pre-heat the oven to gas mark 4, 350°F (180°C). Now separate the eggs, placing the yolks in a medium bowl and the whites in a large, grease-free one. Next, whisk the yolks and the tablespoon of sugar together quite briskly for about a minute, then sift the cocoa powder on to the yolks, whisking briefly until it's well blended in.

Now, using an electric hand whisk, whisk the egg whites to the soft-peak stage; they need to be standing up in peaks that just nod over when you lift the whisk. After that, fold a tablespoon of the egg white into the chocolate mixture, then quickly but carefully fold in the rest. Divide the mixture among the ramekins – it will pile up quite high – then place them on the baking tray and bake for 12-15 minutes, or until they feel springy but still a bit wobbly to the touch. Remove them from the oven, and don't be alarmed to see them shrink because that's quite normal. When they're cool enough to handle, slide a small palette knife around the edges and turn out, first on to the palm of your hand, then right side up on to a cooling rack.

While they're cooling, make the filling. Drain the prunes, reserving the liquid. Next, measure the crème fraîche into a bowl, together with the sugar, then add the prune soaking liquid and whisk everything together before folding in the grated chocolate. Now transfer the prunes to a board, reserving 4 for the tops of the cakes, and roughly chop the rest before folding them into the crème fraîche mixture. Finally, slice the cakes in half horizontally, fill with the prune mixture and sandwich the 2 halves together again. Pop a whole prune on top of each one and dust lightly with cocoa powder before serving.

Chocolate Mousse Cake with Morello Cherries
Serves 10-12

For the filling

8 oz (225 g) dark chocolate (70-75 per cent cocoa solids)

2 large eggs, separated

a 1 lb 8 oz (700 g) jar of pitted morello cherries in syrup

2 tablespoons cherry brandy

8 fl oz (225 ml) double cream

For the base

6 large eggs, separated

5 oz (150 g) golden caster sugar

2 oz (50 g) cocoa powder, sifted

To decorate

3½ oz (100 g) dark chocolate (70-75 per cent cocoa solids) for the chocolate curls (see page 131)

1 tablespoon morello cherry jam

a little cocoa powder, to dust

You will also need a 9 x 13 x ½ inch (23 x 32 x 1 cm) Swiss-roll tin, lined with baking parchment, cut and folded to give a depth of at least 1½ inches (4 cm).

This is an absolute winner - the cake is spread with dark chocolate mousse, filled with morello cherries soaked in cherry brandy, and then topped with soft, curled flakes of chocolate. For chocolate lovers, there's heaven in every mouthful! This is an adult cake and so it works best with dark chocolate that has 70-75 per cent cocoa solids.

You can make the chocolate filling well ahead of time. To do this, break the pieces of chocolate into a basin and add 2 tablespoons of water. Now place the basin over a saucepan of barely simmering water, making quite sure the bottom of the basin isn't actually touching the water. Keep the heat at a minimum and wait for the chocolate to melt. Then remove from the heat and beat with a wooden spoon until smooth. Next, beat the egg yolks – first on their own and then into the warm chocolate mixture. Then, as soon as the mixture has cooled, whisk the egg whites to the soft-peak stage and gently cut and fold them in, too. Cover the bowl with clingfilm and leave it in the fridge till you're ready to use it, but for a minimum of an hour. Drain the cherries in a sieve. Discard the syrup, then place the cherries in a shallow dish, spoon over the cherry brandy and leave aside till needed. Pre-heat the oven to gas mark 4, 350°F (180°C).

For the base, first place the egg yolks in a bowl and whisk them with an electric hand whisk until they begin to thicken. Then add the caster sugar and continue to whisk – but be careful not to overdo this, as it can eventually become too thick, which makes it difficult to fold in the egg whites. Now fold in the cocoa powder. Then, using a spanking clean bowl, whisk the egg whites to the soft-peak stage. Then take 1 large spoonful and fold it into the chocolatey mixture to slacken it, and then gently cut and fold in the rest of the egg whites. Now pour the mixture into the prepared tin and bake the cake on the middle shelf of the oven for about 20-25 minutes. It will look very puffy, but a little finger gently pressed into the centre should reveal that it's springy in the centre and cooked. It's important not to overcook it. Remove it from the oven and don't panic as it sinks down, because this is quite normal. Leave until it's absolutely cold, then turn it out on to a sheet of greaseproof paper, which has been lightly dusted with sifted cocoa powder. Then carefully peel away the paper. Drain the cherries again in a sieve placed over a bowl, to catch the liqueur, and sprinkle all but 1 tablespoon of the liqueur all over the base of the cake. Next, remove the chocolate filling from the fridge and, using a palette knife, spread it carefully and evenly all over the surface of the cake. Now softly whip the double cream and spread this all over the chocolate filling, then lightly press the cherries into the cream.

Rolling this cake up is going to be a lot easier than you think. All you do is take hold of one edge of the paper beneath it and lift it – as you lift, the cake will begin to come up. Just gently roll it over, pulling the paper away as it rolls. If the cake cracks as you roll it, this is not a problem – this can look very attractive and, anyway, it's all going to get covered in chocolate! Now you can decorate the cake. Spoon the cherry jam into a small saucepan, adding the reserved tablespoon of liqueur from the cherries, warm gently, then brush it all over the surface. Place chocolate curls all over that and finally, sift a little cocoa powder to lightly dust the surface.

Note This recipe contains raw eggs.

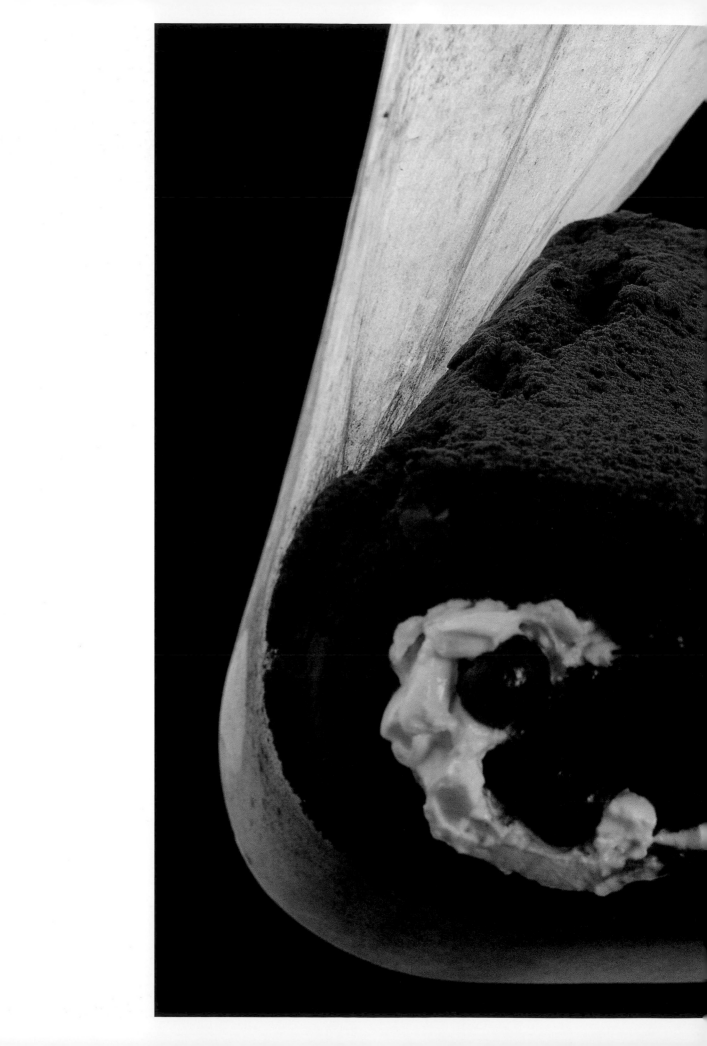

Chocolate Crunch Torte
with Pistachios and Sour Cherries
Serves 12

8 oz (225 g) dark chocolate
(70-75 per cent cocoa solids),
broken into pieces

4 oz (110 g) unsalted pistachio
nuts, roughly chopped

2 oz (50 g) dried sour cherries

2 oz (50 g) raisins

3 tablespoons rum

2 oz (50 g) butter

5 fl oz (150 ml) double cream,
lightly whipped

8 oz (225 g) sweet oat biscuits,
roughly chopped

To serve

a little cocoa powder for dusting

crème fraîche, whipped cream
or pouring cream

You will also need a loose-based
cake tin with a diameter of
8 inches (20 cm), 1½ inches
(4 cm) deep, lightly greased with
a flavourless oil.

This is the easiest chocolate recipe ever invented – I first made a more basic version on children's television. Since then it's got much more sophisticated, but the joy of its simplicity, and the fact that no cooking is required, make it a real winner for busy people.

Begin this the day before by soaking the dried cherries and raisins in the rum overnight. When you are ready to make the torte, place the broken-up chocolate and butter in a large, heatproof bowl, which should be sitting over a saucepan of barely simmering water, making sure the base of the bowl doesn't touch the water. Then, keeping the heat at its lowest, allow the chocolate to melt - it should take about 6 minutes to become smooth and glossy. Now remove the bowl from the pan, give the chocolate a good stir and let it cool for 2-3 minutes.

Next, fold in the whipped cream, followed by the soaked fruits in rum, the pistachios and chopped biscuits, and give it all a good mix. Finally, spoon it into the cake tin as evenly as possible, cover with clingfilm and chill for a minimum of 4 hours.

To serve, dust the surface with a little cocoa powder, cut the torte into wedges, then serve with crème fraîche, whipped cream or pouring cream.

Chocolate, Prune and Armagnac Cake
Serves 8

For the cake

6 large eggs, separated

5 oz (150 g) golden caster sugar

2 oz (50 g) cocoa powder, sifted

For the filling

14 oz (400 g) pitted Agen prunes, soaked overnight (or longer if possible) in 4 fl oz (120 ml) Armagnac (see introduction)

1 tablespoon crème fraîche

To finish

5 oz (150 g) dark chocolate (70-75 per cent cocoa solids), broken into pieces

1 tablespoon crème fraîche

You will also need two 8 inch (20 cm) sponge tins, 1½ inches (4 cm) deep, the bases and sides well greased, and the bases lined with baking parchment.

Pre-heat the oven to gas mark 4, 350°F (180°C).

Here's another 'no flour' chocolate cake – it's simply made with eggs and cocoa powder. If possible, begin this a couple of days ahead, by heating the prunes with the Armagnac and then leaving them to soak up all the delicious flavour.

Start off by first placing the egg whites in a large, clean, grease-free bowl. Put the yolks in another bowl, along with the sugar, and whisk them until they just begin to turn pale and thicken – be careful not to thicken them too much; they need approximately 3 minutes' whisking. After that, gently fold in the sifted cocoa powder.

Next, with a spanking-clean whisk, beat the egg whites until stiff but not too dry. Now, using a metal spoon, fold a heaped tablespoon of the egg white into the chocolate mixture to loosen it up a little, then carefully and gently fold in the rest of the egg white, slowly and patiently, trying not to lose any air. Now divide the mixture equally between the prepared sponge tins and bake near the centre of the oven for 15 minutes. They won't appear to be cooked exactly, just set and slightly puffy and springy in the centre, so when they're taken out of the oven they will shrink (but that's normal, so don't panic). Leave the cakes to cool in their tins, then slide a palette knife around the edges, gently invert them on to a board and carefully strip off the base papers.

To make the filling for the cake, first of all set aside 10-12 of the largest prunes, then place the rest, plus any remaining soaking liquid, in a processor, along with the crème fraîche, and whiz to a purée. After that, transfer the purée straight from the processor on to one half of the cake, placed carefully on to a plate first, then spread the purée over the cake and place the other half on top.

Now all you need is the chocolate covering. For this, place the broken-up pieces of chocolate in a large, heatproof bowl, which should be sitting over a saucepan of barely simmering water, making sure the base of the bowl doesn't touch the water. Then, keeping the heat at its lowest, allow the chocolate to melt slowly – it should take about 5 minutes to become smooth and glossy. Then remove it from the heat and give it a good stir, and let the chocolate cool for 2-3 minutes.

Now take each of the reserved prunes and dip it into the melted chocolate so that half of each one gets covered. As you do this, place them on a sheet of parchment paper to set. Next, stir the crème fraîche into the chocolate, then use this mixture to cover the surface of the cake. Spread it over carefully with a palette knife, making ridges with the knife as you go. Now decorate the cake with the chocolate prunes. Cover the whole thing with an upturned, suitably sized bowl or polythene cake container, and keep it in the fridge until about an hour before you need it.

Amaretti Chocolate Cake
Serves 8

12 oz (350 g) Amaretti biscuits

6 oz (175 g) dark chocolate
(70-75 per cent cocoa solids)

15 fl oz (425 ml) double cream

4 tablespoons brandy

3 tablespoons cider

cocoa powder, to dust

You will also need a 2 pint
(1.2 litre) pudding basin, lightly
greased with groundnut or other
flavourless oil.

Italian Amaretti biscuits are now widely available in supermarkets, as well as delicatessens, and their strong almond flavour is a perfect match with some strong, very dark chocolate.

To start, break up the chocolate into a heatproof bowl, pour in the cream and fit the bowl over a pan of barely simmering water making sure the base of the bowl doesn't touch the water, and leave until the chocolate has melted. Then take the bowl off the heat and, using an electric hand mixer, whisk the chocolate and cream together until you have a cold, creamy mixture.

Next, mix the brandy and cider together and pour into a shallow dish, then dip the biscuits, one at a time, first into the liquor, then into the chocolate cream, and arrange a layer of biscuits in the base of the pudding basin.

Now spread a layer of chocolate mixture over the first layer of biscuits, then repeat the whole process until you have 4 layers. Place a saucer (one that fits inside the rim of the basin) on top of the mixture, put a 2 or 3 lb (900 g/1 kg) weight on top and leave in the fridge overnight.

Before serving, dip the basin in hot water for about 3 seconds and turn the pudding out on to a flat serving plate. Then put the cake back in the fridge for 15 minutes to allow the outside to get firm again, and finally, dust with cocoa powder.

Chocolate Soured Cream Cake
Serves 6

For the cake

2 tablespoons cocoa powder

4 oz (110 g) self-raising flour, sifted

1 teaspoon baking powder

4 oz (110 g) golden caster sugar

2 large eggs

4 oz (110 g) very soft butter

1 tablespoon milk

For the topping and filling

5 oz (150 g) dark chocolate (50-55 per cent cocoa solids)

5 fl oz (150 ml) soured cream

a few walnut halves or toasted chopped hazelnuts, to decorate

You will also need two 7 inch (18 cm) sponge tins, 1½ inches (4 cm) deep, lightly greased, and the bases lined with baking parchment.

Pre-heat the oven to gas mark 3, 325°F (170°C).

This is for people who don't like things too sweet but, that said, if you do, add a tablespoon of sugar to the filling.

For the cake, take a very large mixing bowl, put the flour, baking powder and cocoa powder in a sieve and sift it into the bowl, holding the sieve high to give it a good airing as it goes down. Now all you do is simply add everything else to the bowl and beat thoroughly together with an electric hand whisk for about 1 minute till smooth. Then spoon the mixture into the 2 prepared sandwich tins, dividing it evenly, and bake them side by side in the centre of the oven for 25-30 minutes. Then turn them straight out on to a wire rack to cool for about 5 minutes after they come out of the oven and carefully strip off the base papers.

Meanwhile, make the topping by breaking the chocolate into a heatproof basin fitted over a saucepan of barely simmering water (make sure the base doesn't touch the water), add the soured cream too, and stir, keeping the heat very low, till the chocolate has melted and you have a smooth, creamy mixture. Then remove the bowl from the heat and, as soon as it's cool, use half of the soured cream topping to sandwich the 2 cakes together and spread the rest over the top. Decorate with nuts and store in an airtight tin. I think this one is nicest eaten as fresh as possible.

Squidgy Chocolate Cake
Serves 8

For the filling

8 oz (225 g) dark chocolate,
(70-75 per cent cocoa solids),
broken into pieces

2 large eggs, separated

For the cake

6 large eggs, separated

4 oz (110 g) golden caster sugar

2 oz (50 g) cocoa powder

15 fl oz (425 ml) double cream

To decorate

2 oz (50 g) dark chocolate
(70-75 per cent cocoa solids)

You will also need an oblong baking
tin, 6 x 10 inches (15 x 25.5 cm),
and 1 inch (2.5 cm) deep, lightly
greased, and the base lined with
baking parchment.

Pre-heat the oven to gas mark 4,
350°F (180°C).

This is probably the most popular chocolate cake of my career to date. Great for a birthday, or as a dessert, it is a perennial classic that will never lose its appeal.

First of all, put the chocolate for the filling into a heatproof bowl with 2 tablespoons of water. Place the bowl over a saucepan of barely simmering water and wait for the chocolate to melt, making sure the bottom of the bowl doesn't touch the water. Then remove it from the heat. Next, lightly beat the yolks in a large bowl and then mix them into the warm chocolate. Now let it all cool a bit. Then, using an electric hand whisk, whisk the egg whites in a clean bowl till stiff and fold them in, too. Cover the bowl and chill in the fridge, but for no longer than an hour.

To make the cake, put the egg whites into a large, clean bowl and the yolks into another bowl. Whisk the yolks until they start to thicken, then add the sugar and whisk until the mixture feels thick – but don't overdo it, it shouldn't be starting to turn pale. Now, still whisking, add the cocoa powder. Next, wash and dry the beaters and whisk the egg whites to the stiff-peak stage. Then, using a metal spoon, carefully fold them into the mixture. Pour the mixture into the tin, spread it evenly and bake on a highish shelf in the oven for 20-25 minutes. By that time, the cake will look puffy like a soufflé (it won't look as if it's cooked – but it will be). Remove from the oven and don't be alarmed as it starts to sink because it's supposed to – when it is cool, it will look crinkly on the surface. Then, turn it out on to a piece of parchment paper, loosen the edges with a knife, lift the tin and now peel off the paper. Next, cut the cake in half so you have 2 squares. Take the filling from the fridge, and whip the cream until quite thick. Then, using a palette knife, spread half the chocolate mixture over one half of the cake, and about a quarter of the cream over the chocolate. Place the other half of the cake on top and transfer the cake to a serving plate. Spread the rest of the chocolate mixture on top, and cover the whole cake with cream. Melt the 2 oz (50 g) of chocolate, allow it to cool a little and drizzle it all over the cake.

Note This recipe contains raw eggs.

Sachertorte

Serves 8

For the cake

6 oz (175 g) dark chocolate
(50-55 per cent cocoa solids)

4 oz (110 g) soft butter

4 oz (110 g) golden caster sugar

4 large egg yolks, lightly beaten

¼ teaspoon vanilla extract

4 oz (110 g) plain flour

½ teaspoon baking powder

5 large egg whites

For the icing

6 oz (175 g) dark chocolate
(50-55 per cent cocoa solids)

5 fl oz (150 ml) double cream

2 teaspoons glycerine

2 teaspoons smooth apricot jam

You will also need an 8 inch
(20 cm) springform cake tin,
lightly greased, and the base
lined with baking parchment.

Pre-heat the oven to gas mark 2,
300°F (150°C).

I don't pretend that this is from the original recipe from the Hotel Sacher, in Vienna, where it is supposed to be a closely guarded secret. However, it is a very good variation. In Vienna, slices of Sachertorte are always served with a dollop of thick whipped cream – but I leave that up to you!

Start off by melting the chocolate for the cake. Break it up into a heatproof bowl, then place the bowl over a saucepan of barely simmering water and leave it to melt slowly, being careful not to let the bottom of the bowl touch the water or the chocolate will overheat. While that's happening, using an electric hand whisk, cream the butter and sugar until very pale and fluffy. Now beat in the egg yolks, a little at a time, whisking well after each addition.

Then, when the chocolate has cooled slightly, fold it gradually into the creamed butter mixture and then add the vanilla extract. Next, sift the flour and baking powder together into a bowl, then put it all back into the sieve and sift it into the mixture a little at a time, carefully folding it in with a large metal spoon. When all the flour is incorporated, wash the whisks in warm, soapy water and dry them thoroughly. Next, in a large, clean bowl, whisk the egg whites to the stiff-peak stage, which will take 3-4 minutes, and then carefully fold them into the mixture, bit by bit, still using a metal spoon. Now pour the mixture into the prepared cake tin, level the top and bake it on the middle shelf of the oven for about 1 hour, or until firm and well risen. When it's cooked, allow the cake to cool in the tin for 10 minutes before turning it out on to a cooling rack. Then leave it to get quite cold.

Now warm the apricot jam and brush the cake all over with it. Next, to make the icing, melt the chocolate with the cream, again in a bowl over simmering water. Then remove the bowl from the heat, and stir in the glycerine, to give a coating consistency. Pour the icing over the whole cake, making sure it covers the top and sides completely. Then leave it to set, which will take 2-3 hours.

Chocolate and Almond Cupcakes
Makes 24

For the cakes

4 oz (110 g) dark chocolate (70-75 per cent cocoa solids), coarsely grated

4 oz (110 g) soft butter

6 oz (175 g) golden caster sugar

4 large eggs, separated

4 oz (110 g) ground almonds

5 fl oz (150 ml) milk

6 oz (175 g) self-raising flour, sifted

To decorate

8 oz (225 g) good-quality white chocolate

2 teaspoons liquid glucose

2 oz (50 g) toasted flaked almonds

You will also need two 12 hole patty tins, and 24 paper cases.

Pre-heat the oven to gas mark 3, 325°F (170°C).

These beautifully moist cupcakes are a very chocolatey affair indeed, light in colour but with dark speckles of melted chocolate inside and a white chocolate icing on top.

First of all, begin by creaming the butter and sugar together in a bowl until they're light, pale and fluffy – an electric hand whisk is best for this. Then beat the egg yolks thoroughly together and add them to the mixture, about a teaspoonful at a time, beating well after each addition. When all the yolks are in, lightly fold in the ground almonds, grated chocolate and milk, using a large metal spoon. Now, in a separate, dry, clean bowl, whisk the egg whites till they reach the soft-peak stage, and then fold them into the rest of the mixture gently and carefully so as not to lose all the air you have whisked in. Finally, add the flour – again, folding that in carefully with a large metal spoon.

Next, put 12 of the paper cases ready in one of the patty tins, then carefully spoon half of the mixture in equal amounts into the paper cases. Now place the tin on the centre shelf of the oven and bake the cakes for 15-20 minutes or until the centres are springy when lightly touched. Allow the cakes to cool. Then repeat with the second batch.

To decorate, melt the white chocolate in a heatproof bowl over a pan of barely simmering water, making sure the bottom of the bowl doesn't actually touch the water. Remove the bowl from the pan and leave to cool for about 5 minutes, then stir in the liquid glucose. Now spread a little of the icing on the top of each cupcake and decorate each with a few toasted almonds. Leave to set and then store in a tin till needed.

Chocolate Mascarpone Cheesecake with Fruit and Nuts, served with Crème Fraîche

Serves 6-8

For the filling

3½ oz (95 g) dark chocolate
(70-75 per cent cocoa solids)

9 oz (250 g) mascarpone,
at room temperature

2 oz (50 g) raisins

4 oz (110 g) whole hazelnuts

7 oz (200 g) 8 per cent fat
fromage frais, at room temperature

2 large eggs, at room temperature,
lightly beaten

1½ oz (40 g) golden caster sugar

For the base

2 oz (50 g) whole hazelnuts

4 oz (110 g) sweet oat biscuits

1 oz (25 g) butter, melted

To decorate

3½ oz (95 g) dark chocolate
(70-75 per cent cocoa solids) for
the chocolate curls (see page 131)

1 teaspoon cocoa powder

To serve

crème fraîche or pouring cream

You will also need a 7 inch (18 cm)
cake tin, preferably springform,
3 inches (7.5 cm) deep;
if shallower than this, line the
sides with baking parchment.

Pre-heat the oven to gas mark 6,
400°F (200°C).

This is quite simply a chocolate cheesecake to die for. If you like chocolate, if you like dark chocolate with fruit and nuts, and if you like luscious, velvet-textured mascarpone – need I say more? Before embarking on a baked cheesecake remember that, to prevent cracking, it's best cooled slowly in a switched-off oven. So you will need to make it well ahead.

First of all, place all of the hazelnuts for the base and the filling into the oven and toast to a golden brown; use a timer and have a look after 5 minutes, giving them extra if they need it. Then remove them from the hot tray to cool. Set aside 4 oz (110 g) for the filling. Meanwhile, make the base of the cheesecake by crushing the biscuits in a polythene bag with a rolling pin – not too finely, though, as it's nice to have a fairly uneven texture, then chop the remaining 2 oz (50 g) toasted hazelnuts.

Now tip all the crushed biscuit crumbs into a bowl, then add the chopped nuts and melted butter and mix everything very thoroughly before packing into the base of the cake tin, pressing it very firmly all over. Now place the tin in the oven and pre-bake the crust for 20 minutes. Then remove it and let it cool while you make the filling. Reduce the oven temperature to gas mark 2, 300°F (150°C).

To make the filling, first break the chocolate into small squares. Next, place them in a small, heatproof bowl, which should be sitting over a saucepan of barely simmering water, making sure the base of the bowl doesn't touch the water. Then, keeping the heat at its lowest, allow the chocolate to melt slowly - it should take about 3 minutes to melt and become smooth and glossy. Then remove it from the heat.

Now spoon the mascarpone and fromage frais into a large bowl and whisk them together until smooth, preferably with an electric hand whisk. Then add the eggs and sugar and give it another good whisking before adding the melted chocolate – use a rubber spatula so that you get every last bit of chocolate from the basin – and then lightly fold the chocolate into the egg mixture. Finally, add the raisins and toasted hazelnuts. Now pour the mixture into the tin, smoothing it out with the back of a spoon, then place it on the centre shelf of the oven and bake for 1¼ hours. After that, turn the oven off but leave the cheesecake inside until it's completely cold.

To serve the cheesecake, sprinkle the surface with chocolate curls, dust with a sprinkling of cocoa powder and serve in slices, with crème fraîche or cream handed round separately.

Cookies Muffins

Four Nut Chocolate Brownies
Makes 15

1 oz (25 g) macadamia nuts

1 oz (25 g) brazil nuts

1 oz (25 g) pecan nuts

1 oz (25 g) hazelnuts

2 oz (50 g) dark chocolate
(70-75 per cent cocoa solids)

4 oz (110 g) butter

2 large eggs, beaten

8 oz (225 g) granulated sugar

2 oz (50 g) plain flour

1 teaspoon baking powder

¼ teaspoon salt

You will also need a non-stick
baking tin, 6 x 10 inches
(15 x 25.5 cm), and 1 inch (2.5 cm)
deep, lightly greased, and lined
with baking parchment, allowing
the paper to come 1 inch (2.5 cm)
above the tin.

Pre-heat the oven to gas mark 4,
350°F (180°C).

If you've never made brownies before, you first need to get into the brownie mode, and to do this stop thinking 'cakes'. Brownies are slightly crisp on the outside but soft, damp and squidgy within. I'm always getting letters from people who think their brownies are not cooked, so once you've accepted the description above, try and forget all about cakes.

Begin by chopping the nuts roughly, not too small, then place them on a baking sheet and toast them in the pre-heated oven for 8 minutes exactly. Please use a timer here otherwise you'll be throwing burnt nuts away all day! While the nuts are cooking, put the chocolate and butter together in a large mixing bowl fitted over a saucepan of barely simmering water, making sure the base of the bowl doesn't touch the water. Allow the chocolate to melt, then beat it until smooth, remove it from the heat and simply stir in all the other ingredients until thoroughly blended.

Now spread the mixture evenly into the prepared tin and bake on the centre shelf of the oven for 30 minutes or until it's slightly springy in the centre. Remove the tin from the oven and leave it to cool for 10 minutes before cutting into roughly 15 squares. Then, using a palette knife, transfer the squares on to a wire rack to finish cooling.

White Chocolate Coconut Kisses
Makes 24

For the cakes

2 oz (50 g) shredded coconut
(as long-thread as possible)

2½ oz (60 g) plain flour

3 oz (75 g) caster sugar

a pinch of salt

4 large egg whites

a pinch of cream of tartar

For the topping

9 oz (250 g) good-quality white
chocolate

4 oz (110 g) shredded coconut
(as long-thread as possible)

You will also need two 12 hole
mini-muffin tins, lined with
24 mini-muffin paper cases.

Pre-heat the oven to gas mark 4,
350°F (180°C).

This recipe came about because I was trying to create something white – white cake, white chocolate, white coconut. The only way this could be achieved was with an angel cake mixture – no egg yolks, no butter. The result is so dreamy and light that biting one reminds me of tender kisses.

Light is the word here, so begin by sifting the flour, sugar and salt together 3 times, lifting the sieve high so as to incorporate as much air as possible.

Next, whisk the egg whites in a large, clean bowl, using an electric hand whisk, until they are floppy but not stiff. Then add the cream of tartar and continue whisking until you get quite stiff peaks that stand up when you lift the whisk. Now sift the flour mixture over the bowl and, using a large metal spoon, carefully fold it in, making sure there are no little pockets of flour that have escaped the folding. Finally, fold in the 2 oz (50 g) of coconut. Next, spoon a rounded dessertspoon of the mixture into each muffin case – it should come just above the top. Then bake them on the centre shelf of the oven for about 8 to 10 minutes, or until they're slightly risen, feel firm and are springy when touched with your little finger. They will turn pale gold but that's okay. When they are cooked, remove them from the oven, let them cool slightly, then transfer them from the tins to finish cooling on a wire rack.

To make the topping, break up the white chocolate and place it in a heatproof bowl over a pan of barely simmering water, making sure that the base of the bowl does not touch the water. Then leave it to melt (which will take about 6 to 7 minutes). After that, remove it from the heat and stir until smooth.

Now place the shredded coconut in a bowl and mix it with two-thirds of the melted chocolate. Then spoon the rest of the chocolate over the cooled cakes and make sure it goes right to the edges. Next, using 2 forks, make rough ball shapes of the coconut mixture and place on top of each cake. Then leave them to set for about 30 minutes to an hour, depending on how warm your kitchen is.

Chocolate Orange Biscuits
Makes about 25

3 oz (75 g) dark chocolate
(50-55 per cent cocoa solids),
chopped into small chunks

the grated zest of 2 large oranges,
plus about 1 tablespoon fresh
orange juice

2 oz (50 g) soft butter

3 oz (75 g) lard
or pure vegetable fat

6 oz (175 g) golden caster sugar,
plus extra for sprinkling

8 oz (225 g) plain flour, plus extra
for dusting

2 teaspoons baking powder

You will also need 2 baking
sheets, 11 x 14 inches (28 x 35 cm),
lightly greased, and a 2 inch (5 cm)
plain cutter.

Pre-heat the oven to gas mark 4
350°F (180°C).

I like to keep these in an airtight cookie jar – trouble is, they are never there for long.

Start by beating the fats and sugar together until they're pale and fluffy, then sift the flour and baking powder straight on to the creamed mixture. Next, add the rest of the ingredients, and work the mixture together until you get a fairly stiff paste.

Now lightly flour a work surface and a rolling pin and roll the paste out to between $\frac{1}{4}$ and $\frac{1}{2}$ inch thick (5 mm-1 cm), then, using a 2 inch (5 cm) plain cutter, cut out the biscuits and place them on the greased baking sheets. Sprinkle the biscuits with a little additional caster sugar, then bake them for about 20 minutes, or until the biscuits are a nice golden colour. Take them out of the oven and leave them on the baking sheets for 5 minutes, then cool on a wire rack and, when cold, store in an airtight container.

Florentines
Makes about 20

5 oz (150 g) dark chocolate
(70-75 per cent cocoa solids)

1 oz (25 g) butter, plus a little
melted butter for greasing

3 oz (75 g) golden caster sugar

½ oz (10 g) plain flour, plus extra
for dusting

2½ fl oz (65 ml) double cream

2 oz (50 g) whole almonds,
blanched and cut into thin slivers

2 oz (50 g) ready-flaked almonds

2 oz (50 g) whole candied peel,
chopped

1 oz (25 g) glacé cherries, chopped

1 oz (25 g) angelica, finely chopped
(if you can't find angelica, use
green glacé cherries instead)

You will also need 2 baking sheets,
11 x 14 inches (28 x 35 cm).

Pre-heat the oven to gas mark 5,
375°F (190°C).

These very luxurious biscuits can't be dashed off in five minutes but, if you have the time, then they do make a marvellous present, particularly at Christmas time.

Start by melting the 1 oz (25 g) of butter, together with the sugar and flour, in a small, heavy-based saucepan over a very low heat, and keep stirring until the mixture has melted. Now gradually add the cream, stirring continuously to keep it smooth. Then add all the remaining ingredients, except the chocolate. Stir thoroughly again, then remove the saucepan from the heat and put the mixture on one side to cool.

Next, brush the baking sheets with a little melted butter, lightly dust with flour and then tap them to get rid of the excess flour. You'll find it easier to bake one sheet of the Florentines at a time, so now place heaped teaspoonfuls of the mixture on to one of the prepared baking sheets, spacing them about an inch (2.5 cm) apart (to allow the mixture room to expand while baking). Flatten each spoonful with the back of the spoon, then bake on a high shelf for about 12-15 minutes, or until golden. Then take them out of the oven and leave the biscuits to harden on the baking sheets for 2-3 minutes, before quickly removing them to a wire rack to cool. Repeat with the second batch.

Next, melt the chocolate in a basin over a saucepan of barely simmering water, making sure the base of the bowl doesn't touch the water. Place the cooled Florentines, base up, on a wire rack and, using a teaspoon, coat the underside of each Florentine with warm melted chocolate. Then just before it sets, make a patterned, wavy line on each one, using a fork. Now leave the Florentines to cool completely before packing in alternating rows of fruit and chocolate side up in boxes or tins.

Moist Chocolate and Rum Squares
Makes 9

5 oz (150 g) dark chocolate
(70-75 per cent cocoa solids),
roughly grated

5 oz (150 g) soft butter

5 oz (150 g) golden caster sugar

5 large eggs, separated

5 oz (150 g) ground almonds

9 mini eggs, to decorate
(if you like)

7 fl oz (200 ml) crème fraîche,
to serve

For the icing

4 oz (110 g) dark chocolate
(70-75 per cent cocoa solids),
broken into pieces

3 tablespoons rum

1 tablespoon double cream

You will also need an 8 inch
(20 cm) square cake tin,
generously brushed with melted
butter, and the base and sides
lined with baking parchment.

Pre-heat the oven to gas mark 3,
325°F (170°C).

These are intensely chocolatey and rich and very fattening, I should think! At Easter time, if you gave up chocolate for Lent, they're just the thing to re-initiate you into the whole chocolate experience and you can top the squares with a mini Easter egg.

First, cream the butter and sugar until pale, light and fluffy. Next, lightly beat the egg yolks together and then add them to the mixture, bit by bit. Then carefully fold in the ground almonds and grated chocolate.

Now, whisk the egg whites with either an electric or hand whisk until they form soft peaks – not too stiff – and fold them into the chocolate mixture. Spread the mixture into the prepared tin and bake in the centre of the oven for about 55 minutes to 1 hour or until it feels springy in the centre. Leave the cake to cool in the tin, then loosen the edges and turn it out on to a wire rack and strip off the lining paper, turning it the right way up afterwards. Then sprinkle the surface of the cake with 1 of the 3 tablespoons of rum.

Now put the broken-up chocolate for the icing in a heatproof bowl, which should be sitting over a pan of barely simmering water, making sure that the bowl doesn't touch the water. Then, keeping the heat at its lowest, allow the chocolate to melt slowly, which should take about 5 minutes. When it's melted, take it off the heat and stir in the cream and the second tablespoon of rum. Now spread the cake with the chocolate icing and, if you like, decorate with mini eggs. When the icing has set, cut the cake into 9 squares. Mix the remaining tablespoon of rum into the crème fraîche and serve with the cake.

Chocolate Chip Ginger Nuts
Makes 16

2 oz (50 g) dark chocolate
(70-75 per cent cocoa solids),
chopped into little chunks

a slightly rounded teaspoon
ground ginger

4 oz (110 g) self-raising flour

½ oz (10 g) cocoa powder

1 teaspoon bicarbonate of soda

2 oz (50 g) butter, cut into cubes

1½ oz (40 g) golden granulated
sugar

2 oz (50 g) golden syrup
(about 2 tablespoons)

You will also need an 11 x 16 inch
(28 x 40 cm) baking tray, lined with
baking parchment.

Pre-heat the oven to gas mark 4,
350°F (180°C).

I don't know who invented the expression 'that takes the biscuit', but home-made ginger nuts are, I think, precisely what that expression is trying to convey. Then if you add some cocoa and chunks of chocolate too – well, enough said.

Begin this by sifting the ginger, self-raising flour, cocoa powder and bicarbonate of soda into a mixing bowl. Then, using your fingertips, rub in the butter until the mixture resembles breadcrumbs and next, stir in the sugar and chopped chocolate. Now add the golden syrup, then mix everything with a wooden spoon and finish off by squeezing the mixture together with your hands.

After that, divide the mixture into 16, and roll each portion into a ball. Place on the lined baking sheet, very well spaced out, as they will spread out quite a bit during cooking, flatten each one slightly, then bake on the centre shelf for 15-20 minutes, or until they have spread out and turned cracked and craggy. Cool on the baking tray for a few minutes then, using a palette knife, remove to a wire rack to cool completely.

Chocolate and Prune Brownies
Makes 15

2 oz (50 g) dark chocolate
(70-75 per cent cocoa solids),
broken into pieces

2 oz (50 g) pitted Agen prunes,
chopped and soaked overnight
in 2 fl oz (55 ml) Armagnac

2 oz (50 g) almonds, skin on

4 oz (110 g) butter

2 large eggs, beaten

8 oz (225 g) demerara sugar

2 oz (50 g) plain flour

1 teaspoon baking powder

¼ teaspoon salt

You will also need a non-stick
baking tin, 6 x 10 inches
(15 x 25.5 cm), and 1 inch (2.5 cm)
deep, lightly greased, and lined
with baking parchment, allowing
the paper to come 1 inch (2.5 cm)
above the tin.

Prunes and chocolate are, for me, a heavenly partnership. Plus, if for a special occasion, you soak the prunes in Armagnac, as I have done here, so much the better. These brownies can be served warm as a dessert or just eaten cold as they are.

You need to begin this the day before you are going to make the brownies by soaking the chopped prunes in the Armagnac overnight. So the next day, start by pre-heating the oven to gas mark 4, 350°F (180°C), then chop the almonds roughly, place them on a baking sheet and toast them in the oven for 8 minutes. Please use a timer here, or you'll be throwing burnt nuts away all day!

While the almonds are toasting, put the chocolate and butter together in a heatproof bowl fitted over a saucepan of barely simmering water, making sure the base of the bowl doesn't touch the water. Allow the chocolate to melt – 4-5 minutes – remove it from the heat, then beat till smooth. Next, stir in the other ingredients, including the prunes and Armagnac, until well blended. Now spread the mixture into the prepared tin and bake on the centre shelf for 30 minutes, or until slightly springy in the centre, then leave it to cool for 10 minutes before placing on a sheet of baking parchment on a wire rack and cutting into squares

Chocolate Almond Crunchies
Makes 18

2 oz (50 g) dark chocolate
(70-75 per cent cocoa solids)

1½ oz (40 g) whole almonds,
skin on

4 oz (110 g) butter

3 oz (75 g) demerara sugar

1 dessertspoon golden syrup

4 oz (110 g) self-raising flour

a pinch of salt

4 oz (110 g) porridge oats

You will also need 2 baking sheets,
11 x 14 inches (28 x 35 cm),
lightly greased with groundnut
or other flavourless oil.

Pre-heat the oven to gas mark 3,
325°F (170°C).

Although you can now buy really good-quality biscuits and American cookies, making them at home still has the edge and, as these biscuits are so easy, this is a very good place to start if you are a beginner in home baking. I've used 'adult' chocolate in these, but for children, chocolate chips would do fine.

First of all, using a sharp knife, chop the chocolate into small chunks about ¼ inch (5 mm) square. Now put the butter, sugar and syrup in a saucepan, place it on the gentlest heat possible and let it all dissolve, which will take 2-3 minutes. Meanwhile, chop the nuts into small chunks about the same size as the chocolate pieces. When the butter mixture has dissolved, take it off the heat. In a large mixing bowl, sift in the flour and salt and add the porridge oats and half the chocolate and nuts, then give this a quick mix before pouring in the butter mixture. Now, using a wooden spoon, stir and mix everything together, then switch from a spoon to your hands to bring everything together to form a dough. If it seems a bit dry, add a few drops of cold water.

Now take half the dough and divide it into 9 lumps the size of a large walnut, then roll them into rounds, using the flat of your hand. Place them on a worktop and press gently to flatten them out into rounds approximately 2½ inches (6 cm) in diameter, then scatter half the remaining chocolate and almonds on top of the biscuits, pressing them down lightly. Once you have filled one sheet (give them enough room to spread out during baking), bake them on the middle shelf of the oven for 15 minutes while you prepare the second sheet. When they're all cooked, leave them to cool on the baking sheets for 10 minutes, then transfer them to a wire rack to finish cooling. You can store the biscuits in a sealed container, but I doubt you'll have any left!

Chocolate Mini Muffins
with Toasted Hazelnuts
Makes 24

2 oz (50 g) dark chocolate
(70-75 per cent cocoa solids),
roughly chopped

5 oz (150 g) plain flour

2 tablespoons cocoa powder

1 dessertspoon baking powder

¼ teaspoon salt

1 large egg, lightly beaten

1½ oz (40 g) golden caster sugar

4 fl oz (120 ml) milk

2 oz (50 g) butter, melted
and cooled slightly

For the topping

2 oz (50 g) hazelnuts,
roughly chopped

3 oz (75 g) dark chocolate
(70-75 per cent cocoa solids),
broken into pieces

You will also need two
12 hole mini-muffin tins,
well greased or lined with
mini-muffin paper cases.

Pre-heat the oven to gas mark 6,
400°F (200°C).

The mind-set for muffins is forget everything about cake-making – follow the recipe and don't overmix, remembering it's *supposed* to look like a horrible lumpy disaster so overmixing will spoil it.

You need to begin this recipe by toasting the hazelnuts for the topping. To do this, place the chopped nuts on a baking sheet and toast them in the pre-heated oven for 5 minutes; it's important to use a timer here.

Next, for the muffins, start off by sifting the flour, cocoa powder, baking powder and salt into a large bowl. Then, in a separate bowl, mix together the egg, sugar, milk and melted butter. Now return the dry ingredients to the sieve and sift them straight on to the egg mixture (this double sifting is essential because there won't be much mixing going on). What you need to do now is take a large spoon and fold the dry ingredients into the wet ones – quickly, in about 15 seconds. Don't be tempted to beat or stir, and don't be alarmed by the rather unattractive, uneven appearance of the mixture: this, in fact, is what will ensure that the muffins stay light. Now fold the chopped chocolate into the mixture – again with a minimum of stirring; just a quick folding in.

Divide the mixture among the muffin cups, about 1 heaped teaspoon in each, and bake on a high shelf of the pre-heated oven for 10 minutes, until well risen. Then remove the muffins from the oven and cool in the tins for 5 minutes before transferring them to a cooling tray. While they're cooling, make the topping. To do this, place the broken-up chocolate in a small heatproof bowl, which should be sitting over a saucepan of barely simmering water, making sure the base of the bowl doesn't touch the water. Then, keeping the heat at its lowest, allow the chocolate to melt slowly – it should take about 3 minutes to melt and become smooth and glossy. Now remove it from the heat and give it a good stir, then let the chocolate cool for 2-3 minutes. Next, when the muffins are cool enough to handle, spoon a little melted chocolate on to each one, then place them back on the cooling tray and scatter the hazelnuts over the top of each muffin.

Note For children, muffins can be made with melted chocolate drops and topped with red cherries.

Chocolate Marbled Energy Bars
Makes 16

5 oz (150 g) dark chocolate (70-75 per cent cocoa solids), broken into small pieces

5 oz (150 g) good-quality white chocolate, broken into small pieces

4 oz (110 g) pecan nuts

4 oz (110 g) ready-to-eat dried apricots

3 oz (75 g) raisins

5 oz (150 g) porridge oats

1 oz (25 g) Rice Krispies

1 oz (25 g) Bran Flakes, lightly crushed

1 teaspoon molasses syrup

5 fl oz (150 ml) condensed milk

You will also need a non-stick oblong baking tin, 6 x 10 inches (15 x 25.5 cm), and 1 inch (2.5 cm) deep.

Pre-heat the oven to gas mark 4, 350°F (180°C).

These little bars were originally invented to provide high-energy snack food for footballers and other sports enthusiasts doing hard training. But for strictly armchair sports enthusiasts like me, they go down a treat with a cup of tea on a Sunday afternoon in front of the TV at half-time.

Begin by toasting the pecan nuts on a baking sheet on the top shelf of the oven for 7 minutes, using a timer, then chop them roughly. Next, chop the apricots to the same size as the pecans, and then in a large bowl mix together the apricots, pecans and raisins, oats, Rice Krispies and Bran Flakes. Now, in a small saucepan, heat the molasses syrup and condensed milk until they're warm and thoroughly blended, then pour this mixture into the bowl. Mix it all well with a wooden spoon, then simply tip the mixture into the baking tin, press it down evenly all over and bake in the centre of the oven for about 25 minutes, or until golden brown. After that, leave it to get quite cold.

Meanwhile, melt the white and dark chocolate separately in heatproof bowls set over pans of barely simmering water, making sure the base of the bowls doesn't touch the water. When the cereal mixture has cooled, loosen the edges with a palette knife and turn it out, upside down, on to a board. Now, using a tablespoon, put spoonfuls of the dark chocolate all over the top of the cereal cake, leaving space in between. Then do the same with the white chocolate, but this time fill up the gaps. Next, take a small palette knife and, using a zigzag motion, swirl the two chocolates together to give a marbled effect. Then lift the board and gently tap it down on to the work surface to create a smooth finish. What you need to do now is chill it in the fridge for about 1 hour, then use a sharp knife to cut it into 16 bars.

Maryland Chocolate Chip Cookies
Makes 30

4 oz (110 g) dark chocolate chips

1 vanilla pod

4 oz (110 g) soft butter

4 oz (110 g) light muscovado sugar
or light soft brown sugar

1 medium egg, lightly beaten

2 oz (50 g) toasted hazelnuts,
chopped

3 oz (75 g) plain wholemeal flour

You will also need 2 baking trays,
11 x 14 inches (28 x 35 cm), lined
with baking parchment.

Pre-heat the oven to gas mark 4,
350°F, 180°C.

These delicate cookies are quickly and easily made and taste distinctly better than any shop-bought version. Using ready-toasted chopped hazelnuts can save even more time.

Begin by splitting the vanilla pod lengthways and, using the end of a teaspoon or a small sharp knife, scoop out the seeds. Then, put the butter and sugar together in a mixing bowl and beat with an electric hand whisk until light and fluffy. Next, beat in the egg and the vanilla seeds before adding the remaining ingredients, then stir until thoroughly mixed.

Now take spoonfuls of the dough, sufficient to form small rounds about the size of a walnut, then arrange them, well spaced out, on the baking trays; you will find it easier to bake one batch at a time. Next, bake them on the shelf just above the centre of the oven for 10 minutes or until the biscuits have turned a golden colour and feel firm in the centre when lightly pressed. As soon as the biscuits are baked, remove them from the baking sheets with the aid of a palette knife. Cool them on a wire rack and when cold, store in an airtight container.

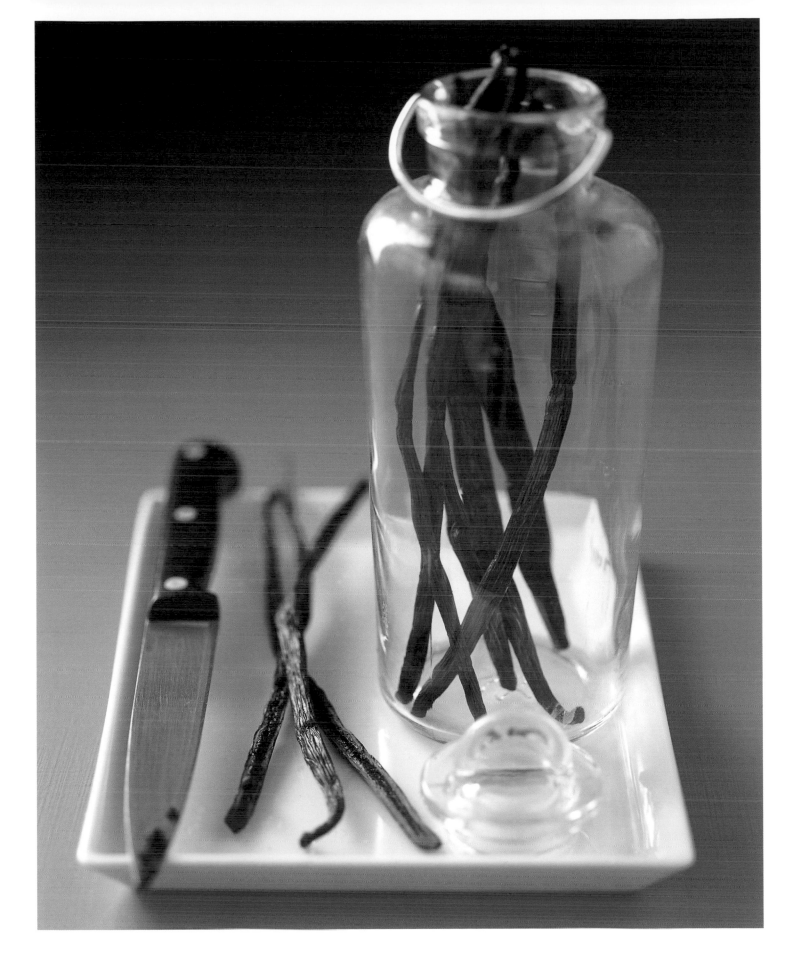

Chocolate Choux Buns
Makes 9

For the choux buns

2½ oz (60 g) strong plain flour

1 teaspoon golden caster sugar

2 oz (50 g) butter,
cut into small pieces

2 large eggs, well beaten

For the mousse filling

6 oz (175 g) dark chocolate
(70-75 per cent cocoa solids)

3 large eggs, separated

For the topping

5 oz (150 g) dark chocolate
(70-75 per cent cocoa solids),
broken into pieces

1 tablespoon crème fraîche

2 tablespoons chopped,
toasted hazelnuts

You will also need a solid
baking sheet, 11 x 14 inches
(28 x 35 cm), lightly greased,
and some baking parchment.

Pre-heat the oven to gas mark 6,
400°F, 200°C.

These lovely, light, airy choux buns are filled and topped with a squidgy chocolate mousse mixture and coated with chocolate icing and chopped nuts.

The mousse filling should be made several hours in advance. First, melt the chocolate in a heatproof bowl set over a pan of barely simmering water (make sure the base of the bowl doesn't touch the water). Then beat the egg yolks into the chocolate and allow the mixture to cool. Now, using an electric hand whisk, whisk the egg whites to the soft peak stage. Stir 1 tablespoon of the egg white into the chocolate mixture to loosen it, then carefully fold in the remainder. Cover the bowl and chill the mousse in the fridge for about 3 hours.

To make the choux pastry, you are going to need to 'shoot' the flour quickly into the water and melted butter, so begin by cutting out a square of baking parchment, fold to make a crease, then open it out again. Sift the flour straight on to the square of parchment and add the sugar. Next, put 5 fl oz (150 ml) of cold water in a medium saucepan, together with the pieces of butter, then place the saucepan over a moderate heat and stir with a wooden spoon. As soon as the butter has melted and the mixture comes up to the boil, turn off the heat immediately, as too much boiling will evaporate some of the water. Then tip in the flour – all in one go – with one hand, while you beat the mixture vigorously with the other. You can do this with a wooden spoon, although an electric hand whisk will save you lots of energy. Beat until you have a smooth ball of paste that has left the sides of the saucepan clean – this will probably take less than a minute. Then beat in the beaten eggs – a little at a time, mixing in each addition thoroughly before adding the next – until you have a smooth, glossy paste.

At this stage, hold the greased baking sheet under cold running water for a few seconds, and tap it sharply to get rid of excess moisture. This will help create a steamier atmosphere, which in turn helps the pastry to rise. Place rough dessertspoons of the choux pastry on the greased and dampened baking sheet and bake on a high shelf for a further 20-25 minutes until the buns are nicely brown and puffy. Pierce the side of each one and put them back in the oven for a further 2-3 minutes to crisp up, then cool on a wire cooling tray. It's best not to put the filling in until about an hour before serving. All you do is slice the choux buns horizontally, but not quite in half, then place a spoonful of the chocolate mousse inside. For the topping, place the broken-up pieces of chocolate in a large, heatproof bowl, over a saucepan of barely simmering water – make sure the base of the bowl doesn't touch the water. Then keeping the heat at its lowest, allow the chocolate to melt slowly – it should take about 5 minutes to become smooth and glossy. Then remove it from the heat, give it a good stir and leave to cool for 2-3 minutes. Next, stir the crème fraîche into the chocolate and spread some of the topping over each bun and finally, sprinkle with chopped hazelnuts.

Note This recipe contains raw eggs.

Chocolate Fruit and Nut Cases
Makes 18

4 oz (110 g) dark chocolate (70-75 per cent cocoa solids), broken into small pieces

2 oz (50 g) raisins

2 oz (50 g) whole blanched hazelnuts (if you don't want to use nuts, replace them with the same weight of dried cranberries or dried cherries)

2 tablespoons golden syrup

2 oz (50 g) butter

2½ oz (60 g) cornflakes

For the topping

18 glacé cherries

You will also need two 12 hole mini-muffin tins, and 18 holes lined with mini-muffin cases.

Pre-heat the oven to gas mark 4, 350°F (180°C).

For absolutely delightful, scrunchy, chocolatey deliciousness, this recipe takes a lot of beating. But that's only half the story. It also happens to be so dead easy that anyone from five to 105 could knock off a batch in no time at all. Glacé cherries are nice for children but you can replace them for adults with a few toasted almonds.

First of all, you will need to toast the hazelnuts on a baking sheet on the top shelf of the oven for 10 minutes, using a timer, then remove them and allow them to cool. Next, melt the chocolate, golden syrup and butter in a heatproof bowl over barely simmering water, making sure the base of the bowl doesn't touch the water. Then, when everything has melted, stir it all together until blended, then remove the bowl and leave to cool a little. Now in a large bowl mix together the raisins, hazelnuts and cornflakes, then pour in the chocolate mixture and do a bit of gentle stirring and folding until the chocolate has completely coated everything.

Now spoon about 2 dessertspoons of the mixture into each muffin case, and top each one with a cherry. Don't be tempted yet! Chill the whole lot in the fridge for about 1½ hours to firm up. If you happen to have any left over, they will keep for about two to three days.

Pudding Hot Cold

Chocolate Bread and Butter Pudding
Serves 6

5 oz (150 g) dark chocolate
(70-75 per cent cocoa solids)

9 slices, each ¼ inch (5 mm) thick,
good-quality white bread, one day
old, taken from a large loaf

3 oz (75 g) butter

15 fl oz (425 ml) whipping cream

4 tablespoons dark rum

4 oz (110 g) golden caster sugar

a good pinch of cinnamon

3 large eggs

To serve

double cream, well chilled

You will also need a shallow,
ovenproof dish, 7 x 9 inches
(18 x 23 cm), and 2 inches
(5 cm) deep, lightly buttered.

I have to thank Larkin Warren, a wonderful American chef, for her original recipe, which I have adapted. It is quite simply one of the most brilliant hot puddings ever invented. It's so simple but so good – and even better prepared two days in advance. Serve in small portions because it is very rich. Though I doubt if there will be any left over, it's also wonderful cold.

Begin by removing the crusts from the slices of bread, which should leave you with 9 pieces about 4 inches (10 cm) square. So now cut each slice into 4 triangles. Next, place the chocolate, butter, whipping cream, rum, sugar and cinnamon in a bowl set over a saucepan of barely simmering water, being careful not to let the bottom of the bowl touch the water, then wait until the butter and chocolate have melted and the sugar has completely dissolved. Next, remove the bowl from the heat and give it a really good stir to amalgamate all the ingredients.

Now, in a separate bowl, whisk the eggs and then pour the chocolate mixture over them and whisk again very thoroughly to blend them together.

Then spoon about a ½ inch (1 cm) layer of the chocolate mixture into the base of the dish and arrange half the bread triangles over the chocolate in overlapping rows. Now pour half the remaining chocolate mixture all over the bread as evenly as possible, then arrange the rest of the triangles over that, finishing off with a layer of chocolate. Use a fork to gently press the bread down so that it gets covered very evenly with the liquid as it cools. Cover the dish with clingfilm and allow to stand at room temperature for 2 hours before transferring it to the fridge for a minimum of 24 (but preferably 48) hours before cooking. When you're ready to cook the pudding, pre-heat the oven to gas mark 4, 350°F (180°C). Remove the clingfilm and bake in the oven on a high shelf for 30-35 minutes, by which time the top will be crunchy and the inside soft and squidgy. Leave it to stand for 10 minutes before serving with well-chilled double cream.

Truffle Torte
Serves 10

3 oz (75 g) Amaretti biscuits, crushed finely with a rolling pin

1 lb (450 g) dark chocolate (70-75 per cent cocoa solids)

5 tablespoons liquid glucose

5 tablespoons rum

1 pint (570 ml) double cream, at room temperature

To serve

cocoa powder for dusting

chilled single pouring cream

You will also need a 9 inch (23 cm) cake tin, lined with baking parchment, and the base and sides lightly brushed with groundnut or other flavourless oil.

This recipe was generously given to me by Derek Fuller, formerly executive chef at the Athenaeum Hotel in Piccadilly, and has proved a winner with everyone who has tried it. It is very rich, though, so serve small portions! The torte does freeze well, but since you can also make it a couple of days in advance, this doesn't really seem necessary.

Start off by sprinkling the crushed biscuits all over the base of the tin. Next, break the chocolate into squares and put them in a heatproof bowl, together with the liquid glucose and the rum. Fit the bowl over a pan of barely simmering water, making sure the base of the bowl doesn't touch the water, then leave it until the chocolate has melted and become quite smooth. Stir, then take off the heat and leave the mixture to cool for 5 minutes or so, until it feels just warm.

Now, in a separate bowl, beat the cream until only very slightly thickened. Fold half into the chocolate mixture and then fold that mixture into the rest of the cream. When it is smoothly blended, spoon it into the prepared tin. Tap the tin gently to even the mixture out, cover with clingfilm and chill overnight.

Just before serving, run a palette knife round the edge to loosen the torte, then give it a good shake and turn the whole thing out on to a serving plate (don't be nervous about this – it's very well behaved). To serve, dust the surface with sifted cocoa powder and, if you like, mark the top into serving sections. Have some chilled pouring cream to go with it; if you have any, a couple of tablespoons of Amaretto liqueur makes a wonderful addition to the cream.

Poires Belle Hélène
Serves 8

8 ripe, firm pears

8 oz (225 g) golden caster sugar

the pared zest and juice of 1 lemon

2 vanilla pods

For the sauce

11 oz (315 g) dark chocolate
(70-75 per cent cocoa solids),
broken into small pieces

7 fl oz (200 ml) double cream

3 tablespoons Poire William liqueur

To serve

15 fl oz (425 ml) double cream,
whipped, and sweetened to taste
with vanilla sugar or good-quality
vanilla ice cream

4 oz (110 g) toasted flaked
almonds, if you like

You will also need a saucepan
with a base diameter of 9 inches
(23 cm).

This classic French recipe comes from a classic French chef, Alain Benech, who brings some French influence into Canary Catering, which is much appreciated by everyone.

First of all, pour 2½ pints (1.5 litres) water into the saucepan, then stir in the sugar, lemon zest and juice, along with the vanilla pods. Bring everything up to simmering point and heat gently until the sugar has dissolved.

While this is happening, using a potato peeler, thinly pare off the outer skin of the pears but leave the stalks intact. Then slice off a thin little disc at the base of each pear so that they can sit upright. Next, carefully remove a little of the core from the base of each pear, using the pointed end of the peeler.

Now put the pears into the hot syrup in the saucepan and cover with a piece of baking parchment, which needs to cover the liquid to make sure the pears are submerged. Simmer the pears in the syrup for 20 minutes, then, using a small skewer, test them to see if they are tender. If not, cook for a further 5 minutes and test them again. When the pears are cooked, leave them to cool in the syrup (they can be stored in the syrup in an airtight, polythene container in the fridge for a couple of days).

To make the sauce, put the chocolate, cream and liqueur into a heatproof bowl set over a pan of barely simmering water (making sure the base of the bowl doesn't touch the water). Stir constantly as the chocolate melts until the sauce is smooth and glossy.

To serve, drain the pears and serve them with the hot chocolate sauce, and some vanilla ice cream or whipped cream. On very special occasions, Alain serves the pears with crème Chantilly – whipped cream, which has been sweetened with vanilla sugar – and scatters toasted flaked almonds over the top.

Iced Chocolate Chestnut Creams with White Chocolate Sauce
Serves 6

For the chocolate layer

3 oz (75 g) dark chocolate
(50-55 per cent cocoa solids)

1 tablespoon rum

2 large egg yolks

1 large egg white

For the centre

a 250 g tin of crème de marrons
(sweetened chestnut purée)

5 fl oz (150 ml) double cream

1 large egg white

For the chestnut layer

a 250 g tin of crème de marrons
(sweetened chestnut purée)

For the white chocolate sauce

2 oz (50 g) good-quality white
chocolate, chopped

10 fl oz (275 ml) single cream

For the decoration

6 marrons glacés
(candied chestnuts), chopped

You will also need six 6 fl oz
(175 ml), non-stick mini pudding
basins, lightly oiled.

This is one of the best frozen desserts ever. Not only do the creams look and taste very good but they are also easy to make and keep well for five to six weeks in the freezer, so that's one party dessert dish that can be taken care of well in advance. I think they look prettiest made in little metal pudding basins, but we've tried them in ramekins and they work well, too. Make sure you use a good-quality white chocolate for the sauce.

Begin with the chocolate layer by breaking up the chocolate and placing it in a small, heatproof basin, along with the rum. Then fit the basin over a pan of barely simmering water; it's important that the basin doesn't come into contact with the water. As soon as the chocolate has melted, remove it from the heat and beat in the egg yolks. Then, using a clean whisk, in another clean bowl, beat the egg white to the soft-peak stage and fold it carefully into the chocolate. Now spoon an equal quantity of the chocolate mixture into each little pudding basin. This, when it's turned out, will be the top layer. Now place the containers in the freezer (I always put them in a Swiss-roll tin for easy management) and leave them to freeze for about 1 hour.

Meanwhile, make the centre by emptying the contents of the tin of chestnut purée into a small basin. Beat it with a fork to even it and soften it up a bit, then, in another bowl, whisk the double cream until it's thickened but floppy; it's very important not to overdo it. Now fold the cream into the chestnut purée thoroughly and evenly until all the marbling has disappeared. Next, wash the whisk in warm soapy water to remove all traces of grease, dry it thoroughly and, in a clean bowl, whisk the egg white until it reaches the soft-peak stage. Now fold it gently and carefully into the chestnut mixture, which will then be ready to spoon over the frozen chocolate mixture in the small pudding basins. Freeze them again for one hour.

Finally, for the chestnut layer, whip the contents of the second tin of chestnut purée and spoon this over to make the final layer. Cover the little pudding basins with clingfilm and freeze until you need them. You can either leave the desserts in the pots or, as soon as they're frozen, turn them out by sliding a knife all around the inside of each container and re-packing them in clingfilm to store without their containers in a freezer box.

To make the white chocolate sauce, gently warm half the cream in a small saucepan. When it's just hot enough for you to hold your little finger in it, remove it from the heat, add the chopped chocolate and stir until it's melted. Then add the remaining cream, cool, cover and store in the fridge till needed.

To serve the chestnut creams, remove them from the freezer to the fridge 15 minutes before they're needed. Then serve in a pool of white chocolate sauce and decorate each with some of the chopped marrons glacés.

Note This recipe contains raw eggs.

Hot Chocolate Rum Soufflé with Chocolate Sauce

For the soufflé

4 oz (110 g) dark chocolate (50-55 per cent cocoa solids)

2 tablespoons rum

2 tablespoons double cream

4 large egg yolks

6 large egg whites

a little melted butter for greasing

a little caster sugar for dusting

For the sauce

3 oz (75 g) dark chocolate (50-55 per cent cocoa solids)

4 tablespoons double cream

To serve

10 fl oz (275 ml) double cream

a little icing sugar for dusting

You will also need a medium baking tray and a 1½ pint (850 ml) soufflé dish.

Pre-heat the oven to gas mark 6, 400°F (200°C).

This is very light and chocolatey, and made even more wonderful by the addition of cream. It is also reasonably well behaved and though it may shrink a little, it won't collapse. It's much better to serve pouring cream with this rather than whipped cream. It's important to use chocolate with a 50-55 per cent cocoa solids content for this recipe, as chocolate with a higher cocoa solids content will make the soufflé too bitter.

First of all, pop the baking tray into the oven to pre-heat. Now break the chocolate into a heatproof mixing bowl, add the rum and cream, and place the bowl over a pan of barely simmering water, making sure the base of the bowl doesn't touch the water. Leave it until the chocolate is just soft, which will take about 6 minutes, then remove it from the heat and beat with a wooden spoon until it's smooth and glossy. Allow it to cool. In the meantime, brush the soufflé dish with melted butter and dust with caster sugar. Now, in a small bowl, whisk the egg yolks thoroughly and stir them into the chocolate mixture. Then, in another large, grease-free bowl – and making sure the beaters of your electric hand whisk are clean and dry – whisk the egg whites until they form stiff peaks. Then, using a metal spoon, mix a quarter of the egg white into the chocolate mixture to loosen it and then fold in the rest gently and carefully.

Next, pour the whole lot into the soufflé dish and bake on the baking tray for about 20 minutes, or until the soufflé is puffy and springy to the touch.

Meanwhile, make the chocolate sauce. Break the chocolate into another heat-proof mixing bowl and add the cream. Place it over a pan of barely simmering water, once again making sure the base of the bowl doesn't touch the water. After about 6 minutes, remove it from the heat and beat it with a wooden spoon until smooth. Pour the sauce into a small jug and keep warm.

Serve the soufflé straight from the oven, dusted with the icing sugar. Hand around the chocolate sauce and cream separately.

Fallen Chocolate Soufflé with Armagnac Prunes and Crème Fraîche Sauce

Serves 6-8

For the soufflé

8 oz (225 g) dark chocolate
(70-75 per cent cocoa solids)

4 oz (110 g) unsalted butter

1 tablespoon Armagnac

4 large eggs, separated

4 oz (110 g) golden caster sugar

a little sifted icing sugar
for dusting

**For the Armagnac prunes
and crème fraîche sauce**

12 oz (350 g) pitted, ready-to-eat
prunes

5 fl oz (150 ml) Armagnac

5 fl oz (150 ml) crème fraîche

You will also need an 8 inch (20 cm)
springform cake tin, greased,
and lined with baking parchment.

Yes, it's really true – this soufflé is supposed to puff like a normal one, but then it is removed from the oven and allowed to subside slowly into a lovely, dark, squidgy chocolate dessert (see picture on previous page).

The prunes need to be soaked overnight, so simply place them in a saucepan with 10 fl oz (275 ml) of water, bring them up to simmering point and let them simmer very gently for 30 minutes. After that, pour the prunes and their cooking liquid into a bowl and stir in the Armagnac while they're still warm. Leave to cool, then cover the bowl with clingfilm and chill in the fridge overnight.

To make the soufflé, pre-heat the oven to gas mark 3, 325°F (170°C). Meanwhile, break the chocolate into squares and place them, together with the butter, in a bowl fitted over a saucepan containing some barely simmering water (the bottom of the bowl must not touch the water). Leave it for a few moments to melt, then stir until you have a smooth, glossy mixture. Now remove the bowl from the heat, add the Armagnac and leave to cool. Next, take a large, roomy bowl and combine the egg yolks and caster sugar in it. Then whisk them together for about 5 or 6 minutes, using an electric hand whisk – when you lift up the whisk and the mixture drops off, making ribbon-like trails, it's ready. Now count out 18 of the soaked prunes, cut each one in half and combine the halves with the whisked egg mixture, along with the melted chocolate. Next, you'll need to wash the whisk thoroughly with hot soapy water to remove all the grease, and dry it well. In another spanking clean bowl, whisk up the egg whites till they form soft peaks. After that, fold them carefully into the chocolate mixture. Spoon this mixture into the prepared tin and bake the soufflé in the centre of the oven for about 30 minutes or until the centre feels springy to the touch. Allow the soufflé to cool in the tin (it's great fun watching it fall very slowly). When it's quite cold, remove it from the tin, peel off the paper, then cover and chill for several hours (or it can be made 2 or 3 days ahead if more convenient). Serve the soufflé, dusted with icing sugar and cut into small slices (it's very rich). To make the sauce, simply liquidise the remaining prunes together with their liquid, place the purée in the serving bowl and lightly stir in the crème fraîche to give a slightly marbled effect. Hand the sauce round separately.

Melting Chocolate Risotto
Serves 6

4 oz (110 g) dark chocolate (70-75 per cent cocoa solids)

7 fl oz (200 ml) crème fraîche

about 1 pint (570 ml) whole milk

6 oz (175 g) carnaroli or arborio risotto rice

1½ oz (40 g) golden caster sugar

To serve

pouring cream

You will also need a shallow, ovenproof dish with a capacity of 2½ pints (1.5 litres), well buttered.

Pre-heat the oven to gas mark 2, 300°F (150°C).

You need to think rice pudding first, then it's easier to imagine a sweet version of a creamy, slightly soupy Italian risotto – only instead of melting cheese you get pools of melting chocolate. Comfort food at its best.

First of all, place the dish in the oven to warm through while you prepare the risotto. Begin by tipping the crème fraîche into a large measuring jug, then make it up to 1 pint 8 fl oz (800 ml) with milk – you will need just over a pint to do this. Now pour this into a large saucepan, add the rice and sugar, then bring it all up to a gentle simmer, stirring occasionally with a wooden spoon.

Meanwhile, weigh out 1½ oz (40 g) of the chocolate and break it up roughly into ¼ inch (5 mm) chunks. Chop the remaining chocolate into little chunks as well, and reserve them for later. When the rice and milk mixture has come up to simmering point, add the 1½ oz (40 g) of chopped chocolate and whisk well until melted and smooth. Now pour the mixture into the warm dish, give it one stir, return to the oven and put a timer on for 20 minutes. After that, give it another stir and time for a further 15 minutes until cooked.

Now remove it from the oven, stir any skin that has formed back into the risotto, then scatter the little chunks of reserved chocolate evenly all over. Cover with a cloth and let it stand for 2-3 minutes while the chocolate melts into little pools, then pour some cream over to mingle with the melted chocolate. Serve at the table in warmed bowls and have some more cream to hand round.

A Very Chocolatey Mousse
Serves 6

7 oz (200 g) dark chocolate (70-75 per cent cocoa solids), broken into pieces

3 large eggs, separated

1½ oz (40 g) golden caster sugar

To serve

a little whipped cream

You will also need 6 ramekins, each with a capacity of 5 fl oz (150 ml), or 6 individual serving glasses.

This was *the* chocolate recipe of the 1960s, which has now, sadly, been eclipsed by other cras and their equally fashionable recipes, but I certainly think it's still one of the simplest but nicest chocolate desserts of all.

First of all, place the broken-up chocolate and 4 fl oz (120 ml) warm water in a large, heatproof bowl, which should be sitting over a saucepan of barely simmering water, making sure the bottom of the bowl doesn't touch the water. Then, keeping the heat at its lowest, allow the chocolate to melt slowly – it should take about 6 minutes. Now remove it from the heat and give it a good stir until it's smooth and glossy, then let the chocolate cool for 2-3 minutes before stirring in the egg yolks. Then give it another good mix with a wooden spoon.

Next, in a clean bowl, whisk the egg whites to the soft-peak stage, then whisk in the sugar, about a third at a time, then whisk again until the whites are glossy. Now, using a metal spoon, fold a tablespoon of the egg whites into the chocolate mixture to loosen it, then carefully fold in the rest. You need to have patience here – it needs gentle folding and cutting movements so that you retain all the precious air, which makes the mousse light. Next, divide the mousse among the ramekins or glasses and chill for at least 2 hours, covered with clingfilm. I think it's also good to serve the mousse with a blob of softly whipped cream on top.

Note This recipe contains raw eggs.

Squidgy Chocolate Log
Serves 8

6 large eggs, separated

5 oz (150 g) golden caster sugar

2 oz (50 g) cocoa powder

For the chocolate mousse

8 oz (225 g) dark chocolate
(70-75 per cent cocoa solids),
broken into squares

2 large eggs, separated

8 fl oz (225 ml) double cream

To finish

icing sugar for dusting

You will also need an oblong tin
6 x 10 inches (15 x 25.5 cm),
and 1 inch (2.5 cm) deep, lightly
greased, and the base lined with
baking parchment.

Pre-heat the oven to gas mark 4,
350°F (180°C).

This roulade again has no flour in it – so it's extremely light and moist. It's also a bit wicked, with its chocolate mousse and whipped cream filling! During the rolling up, it may crack, but this is quite normal and looks most attractive.

Begin by making the chocolate mousse. Place the chocolate in a heatproof bowl and add 2 tablespoons of water. Now place the bowl over a saucepan of barely simmering water for the chocolate to melt, making sure the bottom of the basin doesn't touch the water. After that, remove it from the heat and beat it with a wooden spoon until smooth. Next, beat the egg yolks, first on their own, then into the warm chocolate mixture. Let it cool a bit then, in another grease-free bowl, whisk the egg whites till stiff and fold them into the chocolate mixture. Cover the bowl and chill in the fridge for no longer than an hour.

Meanwhile, you can get on with the roulade. First, place the egg yolks in a basin and whisk until they start to thicken, then add the caster sugar and continue to whisk until the mixture thickens slightly – but be careful not to get it too thick. Now mix the cocoa powder into the egg yolk mixture, then, using a clean whisk and bowl, whisk the egg whites to the soft-peak stage. Next, carefully cut and fold the egg whites into the chocolate mixture – gently and thoroughly – then pour the mixture into the prepared tin.

Bake the roulade on the centre shelf for 20-25 minutes until springy and puffy. When the roulade is cooked, remove it from the oven but leave it in the tin to cool (it will shrink quite a bit as it cools, but don't worry, that's normal). Then, when it is quite cold, turn it out on to an oblong sheet of baking parchment that has been liberally dusted with icing sugar. Peel away the cake tin lining paper from the bottom of the cake (which is now facing upwards), then spread the chocolate mousse filling over the cake. Next, whip the cream softly and spread it over the chocolate filling.

Finally, gently roll up the cake to make a log shape. This will serve 8 people and, although it's unlikely that there will be any left, you can cover any remaining cake with an upturned basin and keep it in the fridge.

Chocolate Crème Brûlées
Serves 6

5 oz (150 g) dark chocolate (70-75 per cent cocoa solids), broken into pieces

1 pint (570 ml) whipping cream

6 large egg yolks

2 oz (50 g) golden caster sugar

1 rounded teaspoon cornflour

For the caramel

2 tablespoons golden caster sugar

You will also need 6 ramekins, each with a capacity of 5 fl oz (150 ml), a plastic spray bottle and a chef's blowtorch.

What chocolate mousse was to the 1960s, crème brûlée was to the 1990s, as it seemed to be on almost every restaurant menu. It's truly a great British classic that easily lends itself to variations like this one – a smooth, velvety chocolate custard topped with a very crunchy caramel. I now use a cook's blowtorch for the caramel, which enables you to get a much thinner layer.

Start the crème brûlées the day before you want to serve them. Place the broken-up chocolate, along with 5 fl oz (150 ml) of the cream, in a large, heatproof bowl sitting over a saucepan of barely simmering water, making sure the base of the bowl doesn't touch the water. Then, keeping the heat at its lowest, allow the chocolate to melt slowly – it should take 5-6 minutes. Remove it from the heat and give it a good stir until it's smooth and glossy, then remove the bowl from the pan and let the mixture cool for 2-3 minutes.

After that, whisk the egg yolks, caster sugar and cornflour together in a separate bowl for about 2 minutes, or until they are thick and creamy. Now, in another pan, heat the remaining cream just up to simmering point and pour it over the egg yolk mixture, whisking as you pour. Return the whole lot to the pan and continue to stir over a gentle heat until it thickens – this will take 2-3 minutes. Next, whisk the melted chocolate and cream together until completely smooth, add a little of the custard mixture to it and continue to whisk it in. After that, add the remaining custard, whisking until everything is really smooth. Then divide the custard among the ramekins, making sure you leave a ½ inch (1 cm) space at the top for the caramel. Now leave them to cool, cover the pots with clingfilm and chill overnight in the fridge. These also freeze well, but do this before the caramel is added.

A few hours before serving the brûlées, make the caramel. Simply sprinkle 1 rounded teaspoon of golden caster sugar over each ramekin of chocolate custard and, using a water spray, first mist the surface lightly – this will help the sugar to caramelise quickly without burning. Now, using sweeping movements, pass the flame of the blowtorch across each brûlée until the sugar melts and caramelises.

Hot Chocolate Fudge Sundae
Serves 6

For the very easy vanilla ice cream

1 pint (570 ml) condensed milk

10 fl oz (275 ml) single cream

14 fl oz (400 ml) crème fraîche

2 teaspoons vanilla extract

For the chocolate fudge sauce

8 oz (225 g) dark chocolate
(50-55 per cent cocoa solids)

a 170 g tin of evaporated milk

For the topping

3 oz (75 g) mixed nuts (pecans,
brazils, almonds, peanuts,
hazelnuts, on their own, or in
combination), lightly toasted
and coarsely chopped

6 dessertspoons whipped cream
or crème fraîche

You will also need a 3½ pint (2 litre)
polythene freezer box, 8 x 8 inches
(20 x 20 cm), and 2½ inches (6 cm)
deep, and 6 tall glasses.

This is the most sublime summer chocolate dessert, especially for eating out of doors - say at a barbecue. The sauce can be made at any stage and kept covered in the fridge, then re-heated.

To make the ice cream, simply put everything into a bowl and use an electric hand mixer to whisk all the ingredients together thoroughly. Then pour the mixture into the polythene freezer box and place it in the coldest part of the freezer. After about 2 hours, or when the edges are starting to freeze, remove it and use the hand mixer to give it another good mix and break down any ice crystals. Return to the freezer, then repeat the whisking after 3 more hours.

Finally, return it to the freezer for a further 6 to 8 hours, by which time it should be at serving consistency. If you've made it a long time ahead and it's very hard, transfer it to the main body of the fridge for 30 minutes to soften enough to scoop.

To make the chocolate fudge sauce, all you do is pour the evaporated milk into a small, heatproof bowl, then break up the chocolate into small squares and add them to the milk. Place the bowl on a saucepan of barely simmering water, making sure the bottom doesn't touch the water, and leave the chocolate to melt, stirring from time to time. It will take about 10 minutes to become a lovely fudgy mass.

To serve the sundaes, put 3 scoops of very firm, cold ice cream per person into tall glasses, followed by 3 dessertspoons of hot fudge sauce, followed by 1 dessertspoon whipped cream or crème fraîche. Finally, sprinkle over some chopped nuts and serve absolutely immediately.

Note Because of the sugar content in condensed milk, this recipe is not suitable for ice-cream makers.

Cheat's Chocolate Trifle
Serves 8

3 double chocolate chip, American-style muffins (about 4 oz/110 g each)

7 oz (200 g) dark chocolate (70-75 per cent cocoa solids)

a 1 lb 8 oz (700 g) jar of pitted morello cherries in syrup, drained and soaked overnight in 3 fl oz (75 ml) dark rum

2 tablespoons morello cherry jam or conserve

9 oz (250 g) mascarpone

14 oz (400 g) fresh ready-made custard

10 fl oz (275 ml) whipping cream

You will also need a trifle bowl or serving dish with a capacity of 4 pints (2.25 litres).

This one's either for people who don't like to cook or for devoted cooks who nonetheless need something really speedy. First, you need to zip round the supermarket to collect the ingredients, then, after the cherries have soaked, this is all made in moments.

It's best to start this recipe the day before you want to serve it, and all you do at this stage is soak the drained cherries overnight in the rum. The next day, begin by slicing the muffins horizontally in half, then spread each slice with some jam and weld the slices back together to their original muffin shape. Now cut each one vertically into 4 pieces approximately ¾ inch (2 cm) wide, and lay these all around the base of the trifle bowl or serving dish. Now take a skewer and stab them to make holes, then strain off the rum the cherries have been soaking in and sprinkle it all over the muffins, scattering the cherries on top.

Now, reserving 2 oz (50 g) of the chocolate for decoration, break the rest up into squares. Place the broken up chocolate in a large, heatproof bowl, which should be sitting over a saucepan of barely simmering water, making sure the bowl doesn't touch the water. Then, keeping the heat at its lowest, allow the chocolate to melt slowly – it should take about 5 minutes to become smooth and glossy. Remove the bowl from the pan and give it a good stir, then let the chocolate cool for 2-3 minutes.

While that's happening, put the mascarpone in a bowl and beat to soften it, then add the custard and whisk them together. Next, whisk in the cooled, melted chocolate, then pour the whole lot over the soaked muffins and cherries. Now whip the cream to the floppy stage, then carefully spoon this over the trifle, spreading it out with a palette knife. Lastly, chop the rest of the chocolate (using a piece of foil to protect it from the heat of your fingers as you steady it), shredding it very finely. Sprinkle the shreds over the surface of the trifle, cover with clingfilm and chill until needed.

Melting Chocolate Puddings
Serves 8

7 oz (200 g) dark chocolate (70-75 per cent cocoa solids), broken into pieces

7 oz (200 g) butter, diced

2 tablespoons brandy

4 oz (110 g) golden caster sugar

4 large eggs, plus 4 large egg yolks

1½ teaspoons vanilla extract

2½ oz (60 g) plain flour

To serve

a little pouring or whipped cream

You will also need eight 6 fl oz (175 ml), non-stick mini pudding basins, generously brushed with melted butter.

These very chocolatey individual baked puddings have a melted fudge-chocolate sauce inside that oozes out as you put your spoon in. My thanks to Galton Blackiston and everyone at Morston Hall Hotel in Norfolk for giving me their recipe.

First of all, place the broken-up chocolate, along with the butter and brandy, in a large heatproof bowl, which should be sitting over a saucepan of barely simmering water, making sure the base of the bowl doesn't touch the water. Then, keeping the heat at its lowest, allow the chocolate and butter to melt slowly; it should take 6-7 minutes. Then remove it from the heat and give it a good stir until it's smooth and glossy.

While the chocolate is melting, place the sugar, whole eggs, yolks and vanilla extract in a large mixing bowl, place it on a tea towel to steady it, then whisk on a high speed with an electric hand whisk until the mixture has doubled in volume – this will take between 5 and 10 minutes, depending on the power of your whisk. What you need to end up with is a thick, mousse-like mixture that, when you stop the motor and lift the whisk, leaves a trail like a piece of ribbon. Now you need to pour the melted chocolate mixture around the edge of the bowl (it's easier to fold it in from the edges) and then sift the flour over the mixture. Using a large metal spoon, carefully but thoroughly fold every-thing together. Patience is needed here; don't be tempted to hurry it, as careful folding and cutting movements are needed, and this will take 3-4 minutes.

Now divide the mixture among the basins (it should come to just below the top of each one) and line them up on a baking tray. The puddings should now be covered with clingfilm and kept in the fridge for a minimum of 1½ hours (it's fine to leave them for up to 8 hours), as it is important to chill the mixture before you cook the puddings.

When you're ready to bake the puddings, pre-heat the oven to gas mark 6, 400°F (200°C). Remove the clingfilm and bake on the centre shelf of the oven for 12 minutes; after that time, the puddings should have risen and feel fairly firm to the touch, although the insides will still be melting. Leave to stand *for 2 minutes only* before carefully sliding a knife around each pudding and then turning them out on to serving plates. Serve absolutely immediately, with some chilled cream to pour over. As the puddings cool, the melted chocolate inside continues to set, so they can, if you like, be served cold instead as a fudgy-centred chocolate cake with whipped cream. These also freeze well but if you're cooking them from frozen, give them 15 minutes' cooking time.

Note This recipe contains partially cooked eggs.

Chocolate Blancmange with Cappuccino Sauce
Serves 8

7 oz (200 g) dark chocolate (70-75 per cent cocoa solids), broken into squares

3 leaves of gelatine

10 fl oz (275 ml) double cream

10 fl oz (275 ml) milk

5 large egg yolks

3 oz (75 g) golden caster sugar

1 dessertspoon cornflour

For the cappuccino sauce

6 slightly rounded teaspoons instant espresso powder

2 fl oz (55 ml) milk

a rounded tablespoon golden caster sugar

10 fl oz (275 ml) whipping cream

cocoa powder, to dust

You will also need 8 mini pudding basins, each with a capacity of 5 fl oz (150 ml), brushed with groundnut oil or other flavourless oil.

I have had a long association with chocolate blancmange: I've always wanted it desperately, but never been able to make it successfully. Then, eureka! It's so simple: make a custard, add melted chocolate and gelatine. The result – absolute perfection, a good texture, the right amount of wobble and a lovely frothy coffee sauce to pour over. You can make the sauce up to four hours ahead and store it, covered, in the fridge.

First of all, put the leaves of gelatine to soak in a small amount of cold water for about 5 minutes. Then pour the cream and milk into a medium saucepan and heat it to just below simmering point. Meanwhile, beat the egg yolks, sugar and cornflour together in a bowl. Then, when the cream mixture is hot, whisk in the chocolate, beating vigorously until the chocolate has melted and the mixture is smooth. Now gradually pour the mixture over the egg yolks, beating as you go. Then return this chocolate custard to the saucepan and place it back over a gentle heat, stirring until it has thickened (don't panic, the small amount of cornflour will keep the mixture stable and prevent it from curdling). Remove the pan from the heat, then squeeze any excess water out of the gelatine and drop the leaves into the chocolate custard, where they will melt in the heat. Give it a good whisk then leave to cool. You can speed this process up by standing the pan in a basin of cold water and stirring occasionally as it cools. After that, divide the cooled mixture among the oiled basins, filling them to around three-quarters full. Now place them on a tray, cover with clingfilm and chill in the fridge for at least 4 hours.

To make the cappuccino sauce, heat the milk and sugar in a small saucepan, then whisk in the espresso powder once the mixture is hot. Next, remove it from the heat and allow it to cool before pouring it into a mixing bowl, then add the cream. Now beat the mixture until slightly frothy and beginning to thicken, then leave it to stand for 5 minutes while you unmould the creams. To do this, ease the cream away from the edge of the basin with your little finger, then invert the basin on to a plate and give it a hefty shake. Using a draining spoon, lift some of the cappuccino 'froth' off the top of the sauce and place a spoonful on top of each cream, then pour the remaining thinner sauce around each plate. Give each blancmange a light dusting with cocoa and serve.

Profiteroles with Hot Chocolate Sauce
Serves 6-8 (makes about 30)

For the profiteroles

2½ oz (60 g) strong plain flour

1 teaspoon golden caster sugar

2 oz (50 g) butter,
cut into small pieces

2 large eggs, well beaten

For the filling

10 fl oz (275 ml) double cream,
whipped until thick

For the hot chocolate sauce

6 oz (175 g) dark chocolate
(70-75 per cent cocoa solids)

You will also need a solid baking
sheet, 11 x 14 inches (28 x 35 cm)
lightly greased, and some baking
parchment.

Pre-heat the oven to gas mark 6,
400°F (200°C).

Profiteroles – little choux buns filled with cream and covered in a chocolate sauce –
make a rather special ending to a dinner party.

First of all, as you are going to need to 'shoot' the flour quickly into the water and melted
butter, cut out a square of baking parchment and fold to make a crease, then open it out
again. Sift the flour straight on to the square of parchment and add the sugar.

Next, put 5 fl oz (150 ml) of cold water into a medium saucepan, together with
the pieces of butter, then place the saucepan over a moderate heat and stir with a
wooden spoon. As soon as the butter has melted and the mixture comes up to the boil,
turn off the heat immediately, as too much boiling will evaporate some of the water.

Then tip in the flour – all in one go – with one hand, while you beat the mixture vigorously with the other. You can do this with a wooden spoon, although an electric hand whisk will save you lots of energy. Beat until you have a smooth ball of paste
that has left the sides of the saucepan clean – this will probably take less than a minute.
Then beat in the beaten eggs – a little at a time, mixing in each addition thoroughly
before adding the next – until you have a smooth, glossy paste.

At this stage, hold the greased baking sheet under cold running water for a few
seconds, and tap it sharply to get rid of excess moisture. This will help create a steamier
atmosphere, which in turn helps the pastry to rise.

To make the profiteroles, place teaspoonfuls of choux paste on the baking
sheet, leaving 1 inch (2.5 cm) between them, and bake on a high shelf in the pre-heated
oven for 10 minutes. After that, increase the heat to gas mark 7, 425°F (220°C) and bake
for a further 15-20 minutes until the buns are crisp, light and a rich golden colour. Pierce
the side of each one to let out the steam, then return them to the oven for a couple of
minutes to crisp up, then cool them on a wire rack.

To make the chocolate sauce, melt the chocolate, together with 4 fl oz (120 ml)
water, in a heatproof basin fitted over a saucepan of simmering water (being careful that
the base of the bowl does not touch the water), stirring until you have a smooth

sauce. Just before serving, split the choux buns in half, fill each one with a generous teaspoonful of whipped cream, then join the halves together again. Spoon or pour the melted chocolate over them and serve immediately.

Note Don't be tempted to put the cream in the profiteroles too far in advance because this tends to make them soggy.

Chocolate Hazelnut Meringue Roulade

7 oz (200 g) dark chocolate
(70-75 per cent cocoa solids),
broken into small pieces

4 oz (110 g) hazelnuts

4 large egg whites

8 oz (225 g) golden caster sugar

1 pint (570 ml) double cream

You will also need a baking tray,
10 x 14 inches (25.5 x 35 cm), and
¾ inch (2 cm) deep, lightly oiled,
and lined with baking parchment,
to stand 1 inch (2.5 cm) proud
of the tray.

Pre-heat the oven to gas mark 5,
375°F (190°C).

When we first put this on the menu at Delia's Restaurant and Bar at Norwich City Football Club, it was one of the fastest-selling desserts ever. Please don't worry about rolling it up – if it cracks, it's quite normal. It's lovely having the layers of meringue and filling providing a contrast to each other.

First, toast the hazelnuts on a baking sheet on the top shelf of the oven for 8 minutes, cool and grind in a food processor until very finely chopped, but do not overprocess or they will turn oily. Now, in a clean, grease-free bowl, whisk the egg whites until they form soft peaks, then whisk in the caster sugar a little at a time. Using a metal spoon, fold the ground hazelnuts into the meringue and spread the mixture evenly in the prepared tin. Bake in the centre of the oven for 20 minutes, cool, then turn out on to a piece of parchment (or greaseproof) paper, slightly larger than the roulade, on a clean surface. Gently ease away the lining paper.

Next, melt the chocolate in a heatproof bowl over simmering water, making sure the bowl doesn't touch the water. Then remove the bowl from the heat and leave the chocolate to cool. Whip the cream and divide between 2 bowls. Reserving 4 table spoons of the melted chocolate for decoration, quickly but gently fold the rest of the melted chocolate into 1 bowl of whipped cream until it looks evenly mixed and mousse-like. Spread this mixture evenly over the roulade to within ½ inch (1 cm) of the edge, then spread the remaining whipped cream over the chocolate mixture.

Now, with the meringue placed long side towards you, and using the paper to assist you, roll up the meringue to form a long log shape (don't worry about the roulade cracking, as it's quite normal).

Make sure the seam is at the base of the roulade and, using a spoon, drizzle the reserved chocolate all over the top, using a zigzag movement. Lift on to a long serving dish and chill in the fridge. Remove from the fridge about 15 minutes before serving.

Truffles Fudge

Chocolate Fudge
with Roasted Nuts and Raisins
Makes 60 squares

14 oz (400 g) dark chocolate
(70-75 per cent cocoa solids),
chopped quite finely

3 oz (75 g) mixed nuts,
such as hazelnuts and almonds

3 oz (75 g) raisins

1½ oz (40 g) unsalted butter

3½ fl oz (100 ml) liquid glucose

12 fl oz (340 ml) whipping cream

9 oz (250 g) golden caster sugar

For the top

4 oz (110 g) good-quality milk
chocolate

You will also need a small baking
tray; a wide, heavy-based
saucepan with a capacity of 6 pints
(3.5 litres); a sugar thermometer;
and a baking tin, 6 x 10 inches
(15 x 25.5 cm), lined with baking
parchment.

Pre-heat the oven to gas mark 4
350°F (180°C).

This is another Canary Catering favourite, which we serve with coffee – it is widely appreciated and we always have lots of pleas for the recipe.

Begin by roasting the nuts. Spread them out on the small baking tray and roast them for 8 minutes, using a timer so you don't forget about them. Then remove them from the oven to a chopping board, let them cool a bit and chop them roughly. Now place them, along with the dark chocolate, raisins and butter in a large, heatproof bowl.

Next, measure out the glucose. (A hot spoon will be useful here – just dip it in boiled water for a few seconds, then wipe it dry.) Place the glucose, cream and sugar in the saucepan over a high heat. (It does need to be a large, wide pan as the mixture will come to a really fast, rolling boil.) Stir everything together until it gets really hot, and then stop stirring because the mixture does tend to catch on the bottom of the pan and you'll stir scorched bits into the fudge.

What you need to do now is insert the sugar thermometer (protecting your hands with thick oven gloves and being really careful not to splash yourself). When the temperature of the mixture reaches 225°F (110°C) – after about 5 minutes – the mixture will look like dark condensed milk. Now remove it from the heat and pour it over the nuts, dark chocolate, raisins and butter, and stir with a wooden spoon until the mixture is well blended, smooth and glossy. (Don't be tempted to add the chocolate and other ingredients to the hot pan – they will simply burn.) Now all you do is pour the whole lot into the lined tin. Then soak the saucepan in hot water immediately.

When the fudge is absolutely cold, cover it with more clingfilm and chill it in the fridge for at least 6 hours or, preferably, overnight.

The next day, melt the milk chocolate in a heatproof bowl over a saucepan of simmering water, making sure the base of the bowl doesn't touch the water. Then turn the fudge out on to a chopping board, discarding the baking parchment, and use a palette knife to spread the melted chocolate over the top. Use a serrated palette knife or a fork to make a ridged pattern across the topping and allow it to set before cutting the fudge into 1 inch (2.5 cm) cubes.

Hand-made Chocolates
Makes 30

3 oz (75 g) dark chocolate
(70-75 per cent cocoa solids)

2 oz (50 g) good-quality
milk chocolate

3 oz (75 g) good-quality
white chocolate

4 oz (110 g) whole blanched
hazelnuts

7 oz (200 g) mi-cuit plums
(or Agen prunes)

2 oz (50 g) shredded coconut
(as long-thread as possible)

You will also need two 12 hole
mini-muffin tins, each lined
with 10 mini muffin or sweet paper
cases, and a tray lined with baking
parchment, plus 10 mini-muffin
or sweet paper cases for the
mi-cuit plums.

Pre-heat the oven to gas mark 4,
350°F (180°C).

People search the world over for the very best chocolates, but there's no need. The very best of all are those freshly made at home. Just the thing to serve with the coffee after a very special meal.

Begin by toasting the hazelnuts on a baking sheet on the top shelf of the oven for 10 minutes, using a timer, then remove them from the oven and allow them to cool. Now break up the 3 kinds of chocolate into small pieces and melt them separately in heat-proof bowls over barely simmering water, making sure the bowls don't touch the water. Then remove them from the heat and allow the chocolate to cool.

Now, using a small, sharp knife, carefully remove the stones from 10 of the mi-cuit plums, leaving them whole. Now, holding each one in a horizontal position, half-dip them lengthways in the milk chocolate and space them out on the lined tray.

Next, stir the toasted hazelnuts into the plain chocolate and pile them, in approximately heaped teaspoonfuls, into 10 paper cases.

Finally, stir the coconut into the white chocolate, divide the mixture into 10, and use 2 forks to roughly shape each one into a ball, then pop into the paper cases. Now leave all the chocolates in a cool place to set for an hour (or in the fridge if you are in a hurry, in which case they will need at least 30 minutes). When they have set, transfer the mi-cuit plums to the paper cases. Serve a mixture of the chocolates with coffee. They will keep in a polythene container in the fridge for up to a week.

Frozen Chocolate Bananas
Makes 12

150 g (5 oz) good-quality milk chocolate, broken into small pieces

2 medium bananas (total weight about 250 g/9 oz)

You will also need a baking tray, lined with baking parchment, and 6 bamboo skewers.

Sounds odd, doesn't it? But you'll believe it when you try it. These are truly sensational – better than an ice cream or a sorbet. First, you bite into crisp frozen chocolate and then meet the beautifully fragrant, iced banana. Heaven.

First, cut each bamboo skewer in half, using scissors, and snip off the sharp point. Now peel the bananas, then, slicing sharply on the diagonal to produce long oval slices, cut each one into 6 (discarding the end bits or, more likely, eating them!). Each slice should be about ½ in (1 cm) wide. Next, carefully insert one end of the bamboo skewer into each one, then place them on the parchment-lined tray and pop it in the freezer for 30 minutes.

While that's happening, melt the chocolate. Place in a heatproof bowl over a pan of barely simmering water, making sure the bottom of the bowl doesn't touch the water. Remove it from the heat and allow to cool.

After 30 minutes, remove the banana slices from the freezer and, taking each one in turn, half-dip them into the melted chocolate, leaving some banana uncovered at the base to give it a kind of two-tone effect. The chocolate will set almost instantly on the frozen banana, so place them all back on the tray and return them to the freezer until you are ready to eat – they can be served straight from the freezer.

The wonderful thing here is that after they have re-frozen, you can pack them in layers between sheets of parchment paper in polythene boxes, and keep them frozen so you have a little stock on tap for whenever you feel like a treat.

Note If you like, after dipping the bananas in the chocolate, you could also dip them in chopped nuts – just a thought (see picture, opposite).

Miniature Choc Ices
Makes 25-30

a 500 ml tub of good-quality
vanilla ice cream

5 oz (150 g) dark chocolate
(70-75 per cent cocoa solids),
broken into pieces

5 oz (150 g) good-quality white
chocolate, broken into pieces

5 oz (150 g) good-quality milk
chocolate, broken into pieces

2 heaped tablespoons shelled
unsalted pistachio nuts, roughly
chopped

2 heaped tablespoons toasted
chopped hazelnuts

You will also need 2 baking trays,
a shallow polythene box
5 x 8 x 2½ inches (13 x 20 x 6 cm),
with a lid, and a 1 inch (2.5 cm)
melon scoop, baking parchment
and about 30 cocktail sticks.

This is an unashamedly fun recipe, great for special parties and at Christmas, or to serve instead of chocolates or mints at the end of a meal. But although it's fun, the choc ices are seriously good to eat, particularly if you buy the best-quality ice cream. I have used three different chocolate toppings here, but to make it simpler, you can use just one.

You need to begin this recipe the night before, so as soon as you get the ice cream home, transfer it to the polythene box and spread it out in an even layer, then put the lid on and pop it in the freezer overnight. At the same time, line the baking trays with baking parchment, place these one on top of the other and put them in the freezer as well.

When you're ready to start making the choc ices, begin by putting a small saucepan of water on to boil. Remove the ice cream and one baking tray from the freezer, then dip the melon scoop in boiling water before making each ice. Just draw the scoop all along the frozen ice cream to form little rounds, and quickly transfer each one to the frozen tray. You do need to work at high speed here, so no distractions, if possible, but if you find the ice cream is getting too soft to work with, just whack everything back in the freezer and continue later. (With no interruptions you should be able to do them all in one session.) Next, insert a cocktail stick into the centre of each ice, then put them all back in the freezer for a minimum of 2 hours, because the ice-cream balls need to get really hard again.

After the 2 hours, melt the dark, white and milk chocolates separately. For this, first place the broken-up pieces of dark chocolate in a large, heatproof bowl sitting over a saucepan of barely simmering water, making sure the base of the bowl doesn't touch the water. Then, keeping the heat at its lowest, allow the chocolate to melt slowly – it will take about 5 minutes to become smooth and glossy. Then remove the chocolate from the heat, give it a good stir and let it cool while you repeat this process with the other 2 chocolates (the white and milk chocolates will take 3-4 minutes to melt). Next, it's very important to allow each chocolate to cool completely to room temperature before coating the ices, or the ice cream will melt. So start off by coating a third of the ice-cream balls with the white chocolate: lift each ice cream up off the tray, using the cocktail stick, and, holding it over a plate, spoon the chocolate over to coat the ice cream completely. Now scatter with a few chopped pistachios (but not over the bowl of chocolate!), then return to the baking tray; you'll find the chocolate will harden around the ice cream immediately. Next, coat a third in milk chocolate, then the rest in the plain chocolate, and scatter these with the toasted hazelnuts. Pop them back in the freezer as soon as you can and serve straight from the freezer.

Other nuts can be used, or finely chop up 4 pieces of crystallised stem ginger and mix with one of the kinds of chocolate before coating the ice creams.

Note If you want to make these a long time ahead, cover with freezer foil.

Truffles
Makes about 36

Basic truffle mixture

5 oz (150 g) dark chocolate
(70-75 per cent cocoa solids)

5 fl oz (150 ml) thick double cream

1 oz (25 g) unsalted butter

2 tablespoons rum or brandy

1 tablespoon Greek yoghurt

For the plain truffles

3 tablespoons cocoa powder

You will also need some paper
sweet cases.

This is a subject that experts get awfully fussed about and there are all kinds of rules and regulations about handling chocolate. Therefore, what I have on offer here are the *easiest* home-made truffles in the world. They will make an extra-special gift for someone who is happy to consume them within three days and they make an equally special ending to a meal – served with liqueurs and coffee. This is the basic truffle recipe made into plain truffles but there are three other variations to try on page 127.

For the basic truffle mixture, break the chocolate into squares and place it in the bowl of a food processor. Switch on and grind the chocolate until it looks granular, like sugar. Now place the cream, butter and rum or brandy in a small saucepan and bring these to simmering point. Then, with the motor switched on, pour the mixture through the feeder tube of the processor and continue to blend until you have a smooth, blended mixture. Now add the yoghurt and blend again for a few seconds.

Next, transfer the mixture, which will be very liquid at this stage, into a bowl, allow it to get quite cold, then cover it with clingfilm and refrigerate overnight. Don't worry: it will thicken up after several hours.

Next day, make sure you have all the little paper cases opened out ready before your hands get all chocolatey! Then, simply sift the cocoa powder on to a large, flat plate, take heaped half teaspoons of the truffle mixture and either dust each one straightaway all over, which gives the truffle a rough, rock-like appearance, or dust your hands in cocoa and roll each piece into a ball and then roll it in the cocoa powder if you like a smoother look. Place the truffle immediately into a paper case. Obviously, the less handling the better as the warmth of your hands melts the chocolate.

Arrange the truffles in a box or boxes and cover. Keep them refrigerated and eat within three days. Alternatively, truffles are ideal for freezing.

Truffle Variations

These are all made from the basic truffle mixture on page 124.

Ginger Truffles

3 oz (75 g) preserved ginger, very finely chopped, plus some extra, cut into small pieces

Mix the finely chopped ginger into the plain truffle mixture, using a fork, then proceed, taking small pieces, rolling or not (as you wish), and dusting with cocoa powder before transferring each one to a paper case.

Toasted Almond Truffles

4 oz (110 g) flaked almonds, well toasted and very finely chopped

Sprinkle the almonds on to a flat plate, then take half teaspoonfuls of the truffle mixture and roll them first into little balls and then round in the nuts, pressing the nuts to form an outer coating.

Chocolate-coated Truffles

8 oz (225 g) dark chocolate
(70-75 per cent cocoa solids)

1 teaspoon groundnut or other flavourless oil

For these you need to set the chocolate and oil in a bowl over some hot but not boiling water and allow it to melt until it becomes liquid, then remove the pan from the heat. Now spread some baking parchment on a flat surface and, dusting your hands with cocoa, roll each truffle into a little ball. Using 2 flat skewers, 1 to spike the truffle and 1 to manoeuvre it, dip each truffle in the chocolate so that it gets a thin coating and then quickly transfer it to the paper. If the chocolate begins to thicken, replace the pan on the heat so that it will liquefy again. Leave the truffles to set, then, using a palette knife, quickly transfer them into the paper cases.

Mixed truffles

Make some plain truffles (page 124) and some of each of the 3 varieties (left). Before you chill the basic truffle mixture, divide it equally among 4 bowls, and chill until needed. Then proceed to use the following quantities for each quarter of mixture:

For the Plain Truffles

1 dessertspoon cocoa powder

For the Ginger Truffles

¾ oz (20 g) preserved ginger

For the Toasted Almond Truffles

1 oz (25 g) flaked almonds

For the Chocolate-coated Truffles

2 oz (50 g) dark chocolate

Chocolate Extras

Chocolate Fudge Filling and Topping

This delicious mixture makes enough to fill and coat the sides and top of a 7 or 8 inch (18 or 20 cm) chocolate cake. Or use it to top 18 cupcakes.

4½ oz (125 g) light soft brown sugar
a 170 g tin of evaporated milk

4½ oz (125 g) dark chocolate (50-55 per cent cocoa solids), broken into small pieces

2 oz (50 g) butter

2 drops of vanilla extract

To start with, combine the sugar and evaporated milk in a heavy saucepan. Now place the pan over a low heat and allow the sugar to dissolve, stirring frequently. When all the granules of sugar have melted, bring the mixture to the boil and simmer very gently for 6 minutes – this time without stirring. Take the pan off the heat, stir in the broken-up chocolate and keep stirring until the chocolate has melted. Finally, stir in the butter and vanilla extract until you have a smooth mixture. Now transfer the mixture to a bowl, cool, then cover and chill for about an hour until it has thickened to a spreadable consistency.

Chocolate Icing

Use this glossy icing to coat the tops and sides of cakes. This quantity of icing will be enough for a 7 or 8 inch (18 or 20 cm) cake.

6 oz (175 g) dark chocolate
(50-55 per cent cocoa solids)

5 fl oz (150 ml) double cream

2 teaspoons glycerine

Melt the chocolate with the cream in a heatproof bowl over some barely simmering water, making sure the bottom of the bowl doesn't touch the water. Now remove the bowl from the heat and stir in the glycerine to give a good coating consistency.

Pour the icing over the whole cake, to coat the top and sides completely. If you have any trouble smoothing the icing, it helps to dip a palette knife briefly into a jug of boiling water and use the knife to help smooth the icing over the cake. Now leave the cake alone, and avoid touching it until the icing is thoroughly set (2-3 hours), or you will spoil the gloss.

Chocolate Fudge Sauce

This is lovely served hot with brownies or poured over ice cream.

8 oz (225 g) dark chocolate (50-55 per cent cocoa solids), broken into small squares
a 170 g tin of evaporated milk

To make the sauce, just melt the chocolate and evaporated milk together in a small, heatproof bowl fitted over a saucepan of barely simmering water (make sure the bottom of the bowl doesn't touch the water) until smooth, stirring now and then. It will take about 10 minutes for everything to melt. Serve immediately, or cool, cover and store in the fridge until you want to re-heat it.

Chocolate Curls

dark chocolate (70-75 per cent cocoa solids), broken into squares
cocoa powder, to dust

As a guide, 3½ oz (100 g) of dark chocolate will enable you to make enough curls to decorate a 7 inch (18 cm) cake.

To make chocolate curls: melt the amount of chocolate specified in the recipe in a heatproof bowl set over a saucepan of barely simmering water (make sure the base of the bowl doesn't touch the water). When the chocolate has melted, pour it on to a flat, smooth surface. It should be about ¼ inch (5 mm) thick. If you don't have a flat, smooth surface, the underside of a large plate will do.

Leave the chocolate to set – what you want is the chocolate to be set hard enough so that if you press the surface of the chocolate, it doesn't leave an indentation. If you use a plate, you can set the chocolate by placing it in the fridge to chill for 45 minutes.

Now use a cheese slicer to make the chocolate curls, or a knife will do if you hold the blade in both hands. Just pull it all along the chocolate towards you and it should curl up. What is very important to know here is that if it doesn't curl and you end up with a pile of chocolate shavings they'll look just as nice – either way, place them in a rigid plastic container and then put this in the fridge until you need them. The curls look lovely dusted with a light sprinkling of cocoa powder.

Conversions for Australia and New Zealand

Measurements in this book refer to British standard imperial and metric measurements.

The standard UK teaspoon measure is 5 ml, the dessertspoon is 10 ml and the tablespoon measure is 15 ml. In Australia, the standard tablespoon is 20 ml.

UK large eggs weigh 63-73 g.

Converting standard cups to imperial and metric weights

Ingredients	Imperial/metric
almonds, ground	6½ oz/185 g
almonds, flaked	3½ oz/95 g
almonds, whole	5 oz/150 g
apricots, dried, whole	6 oz/175 g
butter	9 oz/250 g
cherries, glacé, whole	7½ oz/210 g
chocolate chips	6 oz/175 g
chocolate, grated	4½ oz/125 g
chocolate, chopped	5 oz/150 g
cocoa powder	4½ oz/125 g
coconut, desiccated	3½ oz/95 g
cornflakes	1¼ oz/30 g
flour, plain	4½ oz/125 g
flour, self-raising	4½ oz/125 g
flour, wholemeal	5 oz/150 g
hazelnuts, chopped	4½ oz/125 g
hazelnuts, whole	4¾ oz/140 g
lard	9 oz/250 g
macadamia nuts	4¾ oz/140 g
mascarpone cheese	8 oz/225 g
peanuts, whole	5½ oz/165 g
pecans, whole	4 oz/110 g
pistachio nuts, whole	5 oz/150 g
porridge oats	4 oz/110 g
prunes, whole, pitted	8 oz/225 g
raisins	4½ oz/125 g
rice, arborio, uncooked	8 oz/225 g
Rice Bubbles	1¼ oz/30 g
ricotta cheese	9 oz /250 g
sugar, demerara	8 oz/225 g
sugar, golden caster	9 oz /250 g
sugar, golden granulated	9 oz /250 g
sugar, icing	4½ oz/125 g
sugar, soft brown*	8 oz/225 g
syrup, golden	12 oz/350 g
syrup, molasses	12 oz/350 g
sultanas	4½ oz/125 g
walnuts, halves	3½ oz/95 g
walnuts, pieces	4½ oz/125 g

* Firmly packed

Liquid cup conversions

Metric	Imperial	Cups
30 ml	1 fl oz	⅛ cup
60 ml	2 fl oz	¼ cup
80 ml	2¾ fl oz	⅓ cup
125 ml	4 fl oz	½ cup
185 ml	6 fl oz	¾ cup
250 ml	8 fl oz	1 cup
315 ml	10 fl oz	1¼ cups
375 ml	12 fl oz	1½ cups
500 ml	16 fl oz	2 cups
600 ml	1 pint	2½ cups
750 ml	24 fl oz	3 cups
1 litre	32 fl oz	4 cups

A few ingredient names

chocolate chips
chocolate bits

double cream
thick cream

golden caster sugar
if unavailable, use caster sugar

golden granulated sugar
if unavailable, use granulated sugar

Grape-Nuts
if unavailable, use extra toasted, chopped nuts

ground almonds
almond meal

porridge oats
rolled oats

Rice Krispies
Rice Bubbles

single cream
thin cream

vanilla pod
vanilla bean

Index

Delia Smith is Britain's best-selling cookery author, whose books have sold over 16 million copies. Delia's other books include *How To Cook Books One*, *Two* and *Three*, her *Vegetarian Collection*, the *Complete Illustrated Cookery Course*, *One Is Fun*, the *Summer* and *Winter Collections* and *Christmas*. She has launched her own website. She is also a director of Norwich City Football Club, where she is in charge of Canary Catering, several restaurants and a regular series of food and wine workshops.

She is married to the writer and editor Michael Wynn Jones and they live in Suffolk.

For more information on Delia's restaurant,
food and wine workshops and events, contact:
Delia's Canary Catering, Norwich City Football Club, Carrow Road,
Norwich NR1 1JE; www.deliascanarycatering.co.uk
For Delia's Canary Catering (conferencing and events enquiries),
telephone 01603 218704
For Delia's Restaurant and Bar (reservations),
telephone 01603 218705

Visit Delia's website at www.deliaonline.com